Cork's Rev

By Surreal

About this Book

The third in a trilogy beginning with *The Farmer's Gate*, where the big hearted tarts, Carol and Suzanne, first embroil themselves with Cork.

The story continues with Carol inadvertently booking passage with him on what transpires to be an illegal cruise. *Abduction*

Cork's Revenge details the vicious ex-policeman's continued vendetta. John Cork if ever sane, has finally left the rails. With psychopathic tendencies his only wish in life is to murder Carol.

As the blond sex charity visits her old mate Suzanne, who is nearing the end of her pregnancy, she is blissfully unawares of the trail of butchery Cork is blazing on his path to her front door.

Is this the final episode? Draw your own conclusions.

About The Author & artist:

Older than Methusalah. Wiser than Mike Tyson. Larger than Meatloaf and twice as cuddly. Sexier than Jo Brand. Better looking than Quasimodo. Surreal, happily enslaved in marriage, has a beautiful five year old son and a partner to make the sun shine every day.

There is no horror in the bang, only in the anticipation of it.

Alfred Hitchcock.

NB If you enjoy Cork's Revenge then you'll also enjoy *The Farmer's Gate* and *Abduction* of which this is a self-contained sequel to both. Also by the same author/ artist we also publish *Passion X and* Depravity Road.

Copyright Notice

Figure 1 eBook Cover Picture

Table of Contents

Table of Figures

Foreword

It is with regret that I have to inform you that ISLe has finally lost his marbles. He now languishes in a padded cell drawing graffiti with a child's crayon.

Perhaps he remained too long in chains. Maybe the whip took too big a toll of his wretched body. I don't know.

In his last hours of near sanity he asked me for payment for his work. It was then I realised he had gone mad.

I have no other artist available. So I have attempted to replicate his work. If the drawings do not appease then I apologise. But as someone of importance must have once said, tough!

Surreal

Figure Chapter 1 Reunion

1-Reunion

"Gawd! Look what the cat's dragged in!" howled a surprised Suzie Dixon as she leapt ungainly to her feet, the pages of the 'News of the World' scattering to the richly carpeted floor. Throwing her arms about her life long friend she squealed in delight. "'Ow yer doin' Wyatt Earp?"

Carol Widney caught that embrace and retaliating she countered. "'Ow are yer fatso?"

Suzie held the blond at arm's length. "What d'yer mean, fatso?" she demanded, scowling.

Carol placed a finger on the pregnant woman's distended belly. "I was referring to this bulge beneath yer dress, which looks awfully like quads to me," she explained her smile expanding to a broad grin.

"Nah, there's only one little Bridges in there gel. I've 'ad it checked."

"Big bugger ain't he?"

"He 'as got 'is own swimmin' pool yer knows," Suzie protested, peeved at the loss of her slim waist.

"Got 'is own mansion as well by the looks of it."

Suzie smiled lovingly at her surprise visitor. "'Ave yer come just to insult, or 'ave yer some uvver reason?"

Carol answered tongue in cheek. "I've come to give yer moral support in yer 'our of need."

"It's lack of morals that got me into this state," Suzie retorted. "An' someone's prick shootin' off loose rounds. Talkin' of which, is yer gonna tell me what 'appened wiv Cork?"

Carol's grin evaporated. She turned away. "That were a terrible time Sooze. I ain't sure whether I want to talk about it. Not yet anyway."

That obvious hurt wounded Suzie. Wishing she had not mentioned the subject she apologised. "Sorry gel," she said adding. "I'm 'ere if yer wants to get it off yer chest." The devil returned and she unable to resist, taunted. "Looks like yer needs to get somethin' off it! Gawd Cas! Yer gettin' bigger."

The memory of Cork quickly repressed, Carol retaliated. "You can talk. I ain't never seen yer tits so big. Pot callin' the kettle eh?"

"'Ormones Cas. They'll go down when Zac is born. Mind you, Jeff'll be sorry to see the back of 'em."

"Zac! Zac? What sort of name is that?"

"It's the name of the heir to the Bridges fortune, that's what it is."

"Zac Bridges." Carol tested the name. "'As a certain ring to it, don't it? Bit like Waterloo Bridge or Golden Gate Bridge. 'Ow about Tower Bridges, that's a lofty name?" Both squealed with delight.

"I wanted to call 'im Clifton, but Jeff said the suspense would be too much," Suzie added to Carol's continuous giggles.

Jeff, the father of the butt of their jokes, coughed to attract attention, having until then remained quietly in the background.

"What Jeff?" Suzie asked impatiently.

Timid, he asked. "Sorry to interrupt Suzanne, but are you going to introduce me to your friend?"

"When I'm good and bloody ready!" Suzie snapped. "Now heel boy!"

Much to Carols' amazement, the lad dropped to his knees. "Good God!" she remarked, astounded. "'Ow d'yer get 'im to do that?"

"Simple," Suzie replied. "Whip 'im when he don't."

"That is some'at else. I wish I could've taught bollock chops that trick."

"'Ow is the arse'ole?"

"Nursin' a broken nose last time I saw 'im," Carol replied cheerfully.

"Oh! 'Ow did that 'appen then?" Suzie inquired warily.

"I 'it 'im wiv a mallet," Carol admitted with a sheepish smirk.

"Cor Cas! Did yer gets yer money back?"

"Nah. Fuckin' pig pissed it up the wall before I caught up wiv 'im."

"Bastard!"

"Yeah, he's that all right. Still, that's all water under the Bridges now. An' I got me compensation, so I'm flush again."

"Compensation! What compensation?"

"I can't say too much. There was a reward, well sort of, paid out to do wiv the Pegasus."

"Lucky bitch!"

"Look who's talkin'. Miss millionaire, sometime to be Misses Bridges."

"An' pigs'll fly," Suzie announced disgruntled.

"Yer got to, for Zac's sake," Carol argued.

"That's what I say," Jeff piped up, still kneeling.

"Shut it dog's shite!" Suzie barked. "I might be eight months gone an' the size of a barn, but I can still give you a sound thrashin'"

"D'yer always talk to 'im like that?" Carol asked bemused.

"Even when he's at it gel," Suzie replied with pride.

"But why?"

"Long story. But it's a grand ol' life, ain't it shit face?"

Jeff answered, somewhat forlorn. "Yes Milady."

"Yer what!" shrieked Carol. "Lady? Suzanne Charlotte Dixon a lady? Since bloody when?"

"Since I taught the scivvy the meanin' of obedience."

"An' t' think, I was worried sick about you an' 'im once. I might 'ave known yer'd get the better of 'im. So tell me 'ow." Carol asked intrigued.

"Bad days gone by eh Cas?" Suzie winced, then cursed. "Little toe rag." Smiling again, she rubbed her bloated belly. "'E's gonna be a footballer when 'e grows up. What a fuckin' kick he's got. Where were I?"

"Bad days," Carol reminded.

"Oh yeah. Jeff were missin' a bit of 'is brain when we met. The nice bit. Oh 'e were a savage little cunt then. He tricked me……….."

"Not difficult," Carol interrupted.

Suzie glowered. "As I were sayin'. The runt caught me off-guard. I was mendin' a torn dress. 'Is fault." She stabbed a finger at mister humiliated. "An' 'e throws a rope over me, the shit! Anyways, he leaves me tied up all night and then whips me next day. Gawd that didn't 'alf fuckin' sting."

Carol sympathised. "I knows what yer means."

"Anyways. I thinks he's ninety nine pence short of a pound don't I? Nah he weren't. He were all lonesome and frustrated. Just needed a bit of understandin' that's all. So eventually he comes to trust me, believes I won't do anythin' untoward. That's about it really. He gave me this of course." She patted her stomach. "An' a wardrobe full of clothes of course. An' a 'oliday in Orlando, Florida. An' me bank balance. That's about it really Cas."

"You sure now gel? Not much were it?" Carol ribbed.

"Oh yeah. I did give 'im a bloody good hidin' as well. Yer know for what he done to me. Trouble is gel, he enjoyed it. Bloody twisted little bugger."

"It's a lovely place ain't it?" Carol remarked, changing the subject.

"Weren't always. Right shit 'ole when I first come 'ere. He'd let it go, the lazy b'. Still wiv a lot a 'ard work it came up nice."

"You! 'Ard work?"

"You're kiddin'. It were crap face an' an army of scivvies. Now you gonna tell me what 'appened wiv Cork? And where is 'e now?" Suzie's sensitivity proved short-lived.

"The evil swine's doin' ten to fifteen thank Gawd. They threw the book at 'im. It bounced off 'is thick skull, so they banged 'im up instead. He ain't no worry to me no more."

"Yer all right now then gel?" Suzie probed.

"Yeah fine. I 'ardly 'ave nightmares now."

"Yer shot 'im though, didn't yer? Where'd yer get the gun from? Where'd yer shoot 'im?" Suzie pressed excitedly.

"Oh Sooze!" Carol cried out. "I tried to kill 'im. That's what's so bad. No matter what 'e done, that weren't right. I aimed for 'is 'ead an' 'it 'is shoulder. He won't never use that arm again."

"Not 'is whackin' arm?"

"Nah 'fraid not."

"Shame. Still 'e won't be doin' much of that now, will 'e? An' don't you go feelin' guilty about tryin' t' blow 'im away. 'E got what 'e deserved, trouble is it were a long time comin'. I'd a liked to 'ave done it three years ago."

Suzie glanced at Jeff. "Intro's doggy. Come to Sooze. Lick Suzie's boots. Here boy."

To Carol's utter amazement the lad did just that. On all fours he kissed and lapped at Suzie's feet. "Is he all there?" Carol asked stunned.

"'E's found 'is niche in life. Utter and complete obs......, obseesense......., ob...oh fuck it! He does what I tell 'im to," she proudly boasted.

"Were yer tryin' to say a big word Sooze?" Carol asked, the piss taken.

"Yer cow! I learned it off 'im. It's me state, not my fault me memory's fucked. He's quite clever yer knows. 'E's spineless but 'e 'as certificates. Jeff! Stand up! This is Carol, my bestest ever mate. You be right nice to 'er or else."

Jeff courteously extended a hand. Taking Carol's he stooped and lightly kissed the knuckles saying. "Pleased to meet you Carol. Such a ...." Cut short he winced as a riding crop slashed his backside.

"Yer knows better dog shite! Ma'am! Yer calls her ma'am," Suzie barked.

Jeff frantically rubbed the sting. "Sorry Milady," he pleaded. "Ma'am," he corrected.

With a wave of the hand she ordered callously. "Get out and leave us to talk."

"What a carry on," Carol remarked with the youth gone.

Placing her barely covered butt on a convenient seat she asked. "Is it always like this?"

"Yeah. It's as he wants it. Apparently 'is mother treated 'im like a doormat. He sort of misses that. So if it keeps 'im 'appy.

Even on 'oliday the urge took 'im. Yer'll laugh when yer 'ears this Cas. He says 'e knows this place where we could buy a new whip. So we goes to this cowboy shop.

We's lookin' at a whole load of leather bum biters when this geezer comes over. Big American bloke. All muscles an' 'Ollywood looks. Me fanny fair oozed for 'im, I can tell yer. Anyway 'e says can I 'elp yer like. Yeah I says, I wants one of these, pointing to the whips. Souvenir? He asks in that Yankee Doodle Dandy accent. Nah I says all straight-faced. Me bloke needs correctin'. Yer should 'ave seen Jeff's face! He went puce. This Yank, he laughs. Picks up a real thick bastard and says straight as yer likes, this one'll 'ave 'im dancin'.

Great says I. Touch yer toes Jeff I orders. He gives me such an embarrassed look, 'is face as red as 'is arse was gonna be. Bend over Jeff, I tells him again. So, slowly he does. By now everyone in the shop is watching. The ol' Yank taking it in his stride. I gives Jeff a belter on the butt. Gawd! It must 'ave really stung 'im. Everybody starts clappin'. So bein' the show off I am, I gives 'im another two. It's like one of them rodeo shows; everyone's whistlin' an' shoutin' an' clappin'. A real laugh it were."

"So did yer buy the whip?" Carol asked stunned but not surprised by the account.

"Oh yeah. All lovely and gift-wrapped it were. I towed Jeff out by 'is ear an' everybody was shoutin' things like; give it 'im real good an' see he don't sit down for a week, yer knows."

"Yer 'appy ain't yer Sooze?"

"Yeah. Fallen on me feet ain't I?"

"It certainly seems that way. What about the baby?"

"Over the moon," Suzie confided waddling away for another pee.

Dartmoor: solemn grey walls stood sentinel to the sullen desolation of a scarred winter's landscape. Within those high stone walls lay an isolation wing.

Situated in that dreary barred building, incarcerated in a barren cell six by eight, lay slumped a defeated, miserable specimen of the lower side of human existence.

Curly hair thinning, receding from the brow, a touch greyer then. Eyes staring insanely, sightless. Dribble wetted the jaw. The left arm hung, partially paralysed, as insensitive as the unfeeling wretch attached to it. Cork faced an empty future, devoid of warmth and love: harsh and cruel, synonymous with his nature.

Warden Simmonds, a product of the indulging, rebellious sixties, had misgivings. Cork did not eat. Cork did not wash. The inmate constantly wet his pants, and regularly defecated in them too. This was no proud villain. Not even a conquered rogue lamenting his sins. Cork, said Simmonds, was a sick man.

Psychiatrists asked many devious questions designed to delve the truth of his apparent disorder. Cork did not answer them. Psychologists ruminated and arrived at a solution. Transfer the addled creature.

The final decision. The courts were wrong not to accept his plea of insanity. His crimes were the result of madness and now not properly cared for he had degenerated to the level of a slug.

So arrangements were made. Cork was to be transferred to a secure mental institution. He should be force fed by intravenous drip. The poor wretch had mislaid his marbles. Transport was summonsed to convey the invalid to Broadmoor. One moor to another moor, what more could Cork want? What indeed? Stretched semi-conscious, if conscious be the word for a mindless imbecile, Cork was placed in the back of a modified ambulance. The cab sealed off and mesh welded over the windows.

Alfred Pinge was curtly informed that his prisoner was not dangerous. He had been in a cataleptic state for some weeks and therefore did not require a guard handcuffed to him. Imagine his guardian's face then, when some hundred miles from the prison, Alfred leant to feel Cork's pulse and was faced with the bleak prospect of losing his brains. The talking end of a snub nosed revolver pushed into his nasal opening, Cork's brawny fingers gripping the other end.

"If you wish to see your summer vacation sir, I would suggest you ask your colleague to pull over," Cork imparted in muted voice.

With colour drained, Alfred, ambulance man and hopeful paramedic, called to the driver. "I think you'd better stop George. We have a problem back here."

George Alderman, believing he had a corpse on his hands, not foreseeing there might be two, drew to a halt in a convenient lay-by and mumbling to himself alighted from the cab.

"Didn't look too good when we collected it. Should be a Doc on board. Shouldn't leave it to the likes of us. Ain't fair, anything could happen," he complained, blissfully unawares that anything had indeed occurred.

Dear sweet old George, fifty five next birthday and a grandfather last week, opened the rear doors, his mouth mimicking a letterbox as the terrifying scene sank in. Poor Alfred still had his nose wedged on the gun's barrel. Cork sat quietly, smiled at George. As far as Alderman was concerned, it could have been the devil himself.

"Do come in George," Cork invited with a politeness. "It is cold out there. Shut the doors behind you, there's a good fellow."

Some ten minutes later the demented scoundrel jumped from the vehicle whistling 'Please release me', wearing George's uniform.

The doors re-locked Cork mooched to the front, smashed the CB radio and fired the engine.

The ambulance men stared silently at one another. Both utterly naked, tied with fragmented clothing and air hosing, the butt of a sick joke. Alfred, getting on in years had a bladder problem, he was partially incontinent. Cork, his sadism unvented for eight months had gagged them with each other's underpants. Alfred now eyed his colleague with acute embarrassment as George reaped the results.

Now, where did Cork obtain the gun? The problem with locking such a devious rascal away, is that having served the police force he might know somebody inside intimately. That could work one of two ways. He may have come face to face with one of his arrests and lost all his teeth, (he had a few left.) Or on the other hand he may have re-kindled an old liaison with another ex-copper then serving the prison authorities.

Who knows, perhaps Cork terrified this person with the threat of revealing past indiscretions. After all, why should he serve time while others waltzed free, purely because their crimes remained undetected? This other ex-plod who might have sold on seized drugs may have decided procuring a revolver for an old buddy was preferable to the Old Bailey. Cork certainly didn't buy it from the prison tuck shop.

Surely smuggling in a revolver and keeping it hidden in a cell is highly improbable if not impossible. Maybe, but Cork didn't actually receive it until he was handed over to George and Alfred, that particular guard his escort. Cork had never intended to try and blast his way out of prison. He only wanted the piece if he managed to convince the authorities he was mad.

Chins on fists, bent watching the rain plummet outside; the girls leant on the sill of the living room window. "'Ow d'yer fancy playin' wiv Jeff tonight?" Suzie asked out of the blue.

"Yer what!" Carol cried.

"He needs a good smackin'. I'm getting' that big I can hardly move meself, let alone see to 'im," she explained.

"Gawd Sooze! I thought yer meant ...... yer know, play wiv it."

"Yer can if yer wants to. Yer knows I always shares wiv yer."

"Yeah, like Wayne."

"Didn't 'ave to 'ave 'im," Suzie pointed out.

"That thick cunt cost me," Carol moaned scratching her bum.

"He ain't no cunt. A cunt's useful. Wayne ain't."

"Yer wouldn't be so forward if yer found me and Jeff at it I bet."

"D'yer fancy 'im then? Yer does don't yer?" Suzie scratched Carol's bum.

"Get orf. He's all right, I suppose. I prefer a feller to be a feller though."

"Yer can shag 'im if yer wants Cas. He's a good poke, though I wouldn't tell 'im that. An' at least I'd know where he'd been."

"Is that true love?" Carol asked exasperated.

"Yeah course it is. Love of 'is money."

"Tart!" Carol shrieked.

"Yer better believe it gel. I'm worth nearly three million wiv Jeff. He's moonstruck and I got 'is kid. You tell me any lady of the night that can earn that much bein' poked by all an' sundry."

"So yer are serious about me beddin' 'im?"

"Up to you. He seems seedy, so take yer pill for Christ's sake. Unless yer wants to end up lookin' like me."

"No offence Sooze, but God forbid."

16

Figure Chapter 2 Flip Side

2-Flip Side

A bitterly cold March night, the ambulance jettisoned in a disused quarry entrance, engine running, heater full blast, Cork rifled the stolen wallets of George and Alfred.

"Miserable, penniless bastards," he bitched. "Fifteen pounds and thirty two pence between them. Bollocks! This won't get me to London to see the queen. The queen of tarts." He laughed, the mirth of a lunatic.

Cork checked for plastic, unearthing a building society card. *'Perhaps,'* he thought. Sure enough, Alfred had a poor memory as well as a weak bladder; the pin number was secreted in the back of the wallet.

"Well, well, well," Cork mused. "Three holes in a scrubber. Carol Anne prepare to meet thy maker, eventually!" A vicious smirk twisted his features. Cork started to walk; an early frost crystallised the surrounding countryside.

The fugitive had dumped the ambulance at Runfold near Farnham, Surrey. A steady stride brought him into Farnham centre some two hours later. Cold and hungry he visited a Link machine withdrawing all he could, two hundred and fifty pounds.

With pen and paper, found in the jacket he wore, he wrote out an I.O.U. for two hundred and sixty five pounds and thirty-two pence, adding. 'Thank you Alfred, be rest assured that it will be used in an excellent cause.' On the reverse he wrote. 'Stolen ambulance in Runfold sand quarry.' Cork did not expect it to remain unnoticed that long but did not want two stiffs on his tab, not yet. He believed the police would hunt him with far more vigour if they died. He posted the note and wallets through the building society letterbox.

It was nine thirty by then. Cork needed to clear Farnham quickly and in the not too distant future, eat.

A nearby taxi rank provided the means. Climbing in the back of a white Toyota, he asked the driver. "What's the next major town heading toward London?"

"Aldershot mate," came the reply.

"And after that?"

"Farnborough."

"Is there a fast food outlet there?" Cork inquired, his stomach believing his throat cut.

"Yes mate. A Macdonalds at Farnborough Park."

"Then that is your destination." Cork sank back into the plush upholstery and closed his eyes. Migraine, that scourge of the mind began to envelop him.

"Just off duty are you?" the taxi driver asked, making conversation.

"Yes," Cork replied. "Late shift."

"You driving the geriatrics then?"

"Beg your pardon?"

"Farnham hospital. The old and not all there."

"Oh, yes."

"New to the area are you?"

"Yes. Yes I am."

"I reckon you do a good job."

"Eh?" The head began to pound.

"Ambulance. That's what you do, ain't it?"

"That's right." Cork was in no mood for idle chit-chat, but he didn't wish to be remembered either.

The taxi had just navigated the Clockhouse roundabout on the A325 when a collision occurred a hundred yards in front of them. The road temporarily blocked, the taxi ground to a halt.

"I'll see if they need any help." The driver disappeared, returning seconds later yelling. "There's a woman in there having a baby. Quick mate give her a hand, I'll radio for an ambulance."

Cork sat bolt upright. "Me?" he asked.

"Yeah. You've been trained ain't you?"

"I'm a driver," he blurted.

"Oh come on, don't be modest. Help her for Christ's sake." The man stared, waiting.

"Control." He spoke with an urgency into the CB "Control. Twenty-two fox trot. Need an ambulance at Ham and Blackbird, Farnborough Road. Collision and a woman having a baby."

"You going then?" he asked Cork.

"No not you love. Luckily we've got a medic here. A fare, yeah."

No choice. Cork had gained the requisite experience in the police force. But with a thumping headache and being on the run, he thought his attendance unwise. He had no choice though.

He nosed in the rear of the damaged car. The husband he assumed, started babbling. "It's coming. She's having it. I was in a rush. The bloke in front pulled up too sharp. A dog ran out. I couldn't stop. Oh God! Will she be okay? Thank God you're here."

Cork's head smashed, his stomach lurched, the irritating voice an aggravation he could do without. He glared at the man, then with suppressed temper hissed. "Be quiet!" The husband's mouth snapped shut, as if by a powerful spring.

"Now dear lady, your contractions. How far apart?"

"They're almost continuous." She grimaced; sweat dampened her young face.

"Waters broke?" he asked with no trace of nerves.

"Yeah. Ten minutes since."

"Baby's on the way then. That's not a problem. The whipper-snapper's coming, don't really matter where. It'll all be the same to you." Cork calmed her. Something in his mien spread confidence. That was the better side of a brutal man. He had no axe to grind there.

He helped the woman to lay down on the back seat, supporting her head with her husband's lap and removed her underwear. Calmly he arranged her legs so her heels almost tucked to her bottom.

"Breathing," he said. "You've been shown how I take it?" She nodded. "Deep breath. Push!"

"Oh God! It hurts."

"Of course it does. Life hurts. Baby and pain go hand in hand. You'll forget it soon enough. When you're cradling your healthy new born. Then you'll suffer the pain of love, a love that'll bind you for the rest of your days, no matter what. Now push!"

She squealed.

"Push from your gut. Baby needs your help. He's longing to take his first sweet smell of life. Now push!"

Way off, distant in the freezing night air, the sound of a siren heralded the approach of officialdom. Ambulance he hoped. The police he could do without. If they had discovered the naked inept duo then they could well be looking for him. He stayed put, consumed by the imminence of birth.

"Push! Breathe! Push!" As the wet crown of hair became visible, reaching out through the vagina, like a tennis ball from a sock, the blue flashing light of an ambulance fast approached, evoking a flickering illumination within the car's interior, imitating multi lightning strikes, devoid of thunder.

As the medical team arrived and the engine revs died, so Cork collected up the new-born which had unceremoniously slid from the warmth of her mother to gulp the first breath.

Cork offered the child to the panting, laughing, crying mother, forgotten moisture wetting his eyes. "A girl," he whispered. "A healthy, beautiful baby girl."

As the woman received her child, her own tears flowing with pride, Cork bent to her and kissed her forehead. "May she bring you every joy," he said turning to leave.

"Your name?" the woman called after him.

"He smiled back at her. "John. John Michael Cork," he said. "But please, don't tell anyone else." She nodded. So Anthea J.M. Rayburn had been brought into the world. She would hear someday from her mother why she was called so.

Karen Rayburn kept her word. She had been certain she had seen the grip of a pistol protruding from Cork's trouser waistband. Why he wished to remain anonymous was his business. She was not about to cause trouble for the man that delivered her baby, no matter what.

A green coated paramedic patted Cork on the back. "Well done," he applauded, adding. "Not going are you?"

"Have to," Cork replied. "I'm late for a date."

Back in the taxi he told the driver to forget Macdonalds, he had no time for that then. "Is there a chippy close by?" he asked.

"Yeah. Frimley high street."

"And a railway station? I have to go to London," Cork said.

"Nearly opposite."

"Good. Take me there." Then as an afterthought he asked. "You weren't running the meter while I was delivering that baby I hope."

"Don't worry mate. The ride's on the firm. For what you done."

Cork relaxed, the migraine had dispersed. *'For every one born,'* he mused. *'One dies. Enjoy your last days Carol Anne.'*

Figure Chapter 3 That Loving Feeling

3-That Loving Feeling

More than two hundred miles away and in the opposite direction, Cork's quarry was about to undertake some serious flagellation.

Jeff had been dragged in an apprehensive state by the scheming pair, to a purpose built disciplinary cell; the old attic room was in disuse, too many stairs the pregnant Suzanne had bitched. This one was on the ground floor, at the rear of the building.

Well equipped? When one had money procurement came easy. The walls were mirrored, as was the ceiling. The room measured a spacious thirty by twenty feet, ample room to swing a cat, especially a knotted one.

Those tigresses assaulted the lucky lad, virtually ripping the clothes from his muscled body. Giggling hysterically they debagged him, the threesome a knot of writhing bodies. Jeff feigned resistance, careful not to overdo it.

Face down, hands desperately clutching his underpants whilst Suzie frantically tugged in the opposite direction, Jeff's head came between Carol's stockinged thighs. She squeezed him, his nose an inch from her cotton covered bush, the short skirt ridden high.

"Gotcha!" she squealed.

Face flushed from spent energies he did little to fight free. Instead, mind on other matters he permitted the underwear its freedom, Suzie baring his arse in triumph.

"Nice bum Jeff," Carol remarked in taunting tone.

The lad reciprocated by wriggling until his nose pressed to the soft mound, the sweet smell of her pleasure centre pervading his senses. He kissed that mons.

Carol pulled him closer, he barely able to breath. "Yer got 'im well trained ain't yer?" she said to Suzie. "He seems to know what a girl likes."

"He'll get a smackin' I knows that. Takin' liberties," Suzie threatened scowling. She slapped his bared bottom, a sound wallop. "Get yer 'ead out a there pig's shite. Yer ain't bin invited."

Jeff tried in vain, the more he wriggled the harder Carol pressed her thighs to him, preventing his half-hearted withdrawal. Suzie slapped him again, harder. He squirmed. Carol tensed. Suzie whacked.

His backside hot, burning, scarlet, Suzie proceeded to handcuff him, arms behind his back. She fettered an ankle, then drew his feet towards the wrists, his legs bending at the knees. Suzie passed the links about the wrist's cuffs and secured the free manacle to the other ankle, leaving Jeff hog-tied.

"Now arsehole," Suzie scolded. "Yer can stay like that until Cas decides to punish yer." They left him there to anticipate, the floor tiles cold to his body.

Carol sipped the freshly brewed percolated coffee, laced with cream and brandy. "I ain't sure about none of this Sooze," she confessed.

Suzie's dark brown eyes peered amused, the coffee cup obscuring her mouth. "Why gel?"

"He's your feller. What you're proposin' is all a bit intimate."

"Cas."

"What?"

"D'yer remember our 'oliday in Cornwall? When we met Eric."

"I can 'ardly ever forget, can I? That's when I first came up against Cork."

"Yeah I know gel. But do yer remember what we did down there. Just you an' I, in that poxy tent?"

"Course I do. Yer still got it?"

"What?"

"That fuckin' great pink dildo."

"Nah. Chucked it."

"Shame."

"Not really," Suzanne grinned, a face full of mischief. "I got a great big black one now. Wiv thumpin' great bollocks."

"Yer bugger! Anyway what's yer point?"

"D'yer fancy doin' that again. Cos I do. 'Cept this time we got ourselves a real prick."

"Jeff yer mean?"

"Course."

"A threesome?"

"Yeah."

"Yer means yer wants me to kiss yer?" Carol asked sensuously.

"Yeah."

"Undo yer blouse an' slide me 'and inside?"

"Yeah."

"To ease yer little tit out and play wiv yer nipple?"

"Yeah."

"To kiss that sweet teat and suckle yer boob?"

"Yeah."

"To slide me 'and down inside yer knickers?"

"Yeah. Oh yeah."

"To drop to me knees, ease them panties down and kiss yer curly pussy?"

"Oh Gawd Cas! Yeah."

"To slide me long tongue in between yer tight cunt lips, and lick yer until yer writhe wiv exquisite pleasure."

"Oh please Cas."

"Nah. That's a crappy idea."

"Yer bitch!"

"If yer wants me body, yer can 'ave it gel. Happily. Yer knows I loves yer. I'm just not sure about the threesome that's all."

"Oh Cas! It'll be a laugh. Go on. If yer don't I'll smack yer bum."

"I wouldn't try it. Not in your state."

"Oh please Cas." Suzie begged.

"I thought women in your condition went off it?"

"I don't think I ever will. I needs a cuddle. Please Cas."

"Oh all right." Carol gave grudgingly.

"A threesome?"

"Yeah. Go on." Suzie threw her arms about Carol and kissed her, a passionate mouth to mouth. Breaking free Carol asked. "So anyway, what d'yer want me to do to 'im?"

"Depends on what yer fancy."

"I dunno gel. I ain't really into this sort of lark."

"I made 'im pick 'iself a nice birch bundle yesterday. It's soaking in a bucket. Give 'im an 'iding wiv that," she suggested. "D'yer want to get dressed up?" Suzie asked as an afterthought.

"I am," Carol answered miffed.

"Nah. I mean for the part. It's like acting. Yer plays a part, yer knows, strict madam per'aps. Police woman or prison warder. 'E just loves a uniform. It'll get 'im all aroused, bring 'is tool to attention, juice 'im up."

Carol considered the proposal. "Oh go on then. Might as well do it proper I s'pose. What yer got?"

Jeff had collected a wardrobe of intimate and fancy dress, all Suzanne size.

"I'll never get them around my waist," Carol evinced, examining the skirts. "You were a good two inches smaller, for all your hips."

"Whad'yer mean for all my 'ips. Anyway yer wasn't always bigger than me. Which means." She jabbed Carol's stomach. "Yer's gettin' paunchy."

"Nothin' compared to you," Carol riposted.

"I got a reason," Suzie cried indignant.

"So 'ave I."

"Oh yeah, what?"

"Gluttony." They both giggled, behaving like silly irresponsible schoolgirls.

Carol became serious. "Sooze. I ain't bin wiv no one since that awful time," she confessed.

"Yer kiddin'!"

"Sooze. I were raped." Tears welled, her lips trembled.

"Oh Gawd no! Who? Cork?" Suzanne asked horrified.

"Yeah. 'Im an' three others."

"No wonder yer shot the cunt."

"Sooze, a lot of it were covered up. It weren't only Cork I done. There was three others and the first mate as well."

"Fuck me! A right ol' Annie Oakley weren't yer?"

"I'd 'ave shot all the mother fuckers if old Cookie 'adn't 'ave stopped me."

"Yer never did say gel. Where'd yer get the gun from?"

"It were Cookie's. An heirloom. Big old bastard it were. Yer should 'ave seen their wounds. It were 'orrible Sooze. I just spaced out. I was so full of 'ate. Lucky I was let off really."

"Yeah, 'ow comes yer was?" Suzie asked, her curiosity aroused.

"There were these two government agents aboard. Apparently I saved their lives by what I done. And it seems a lot of uvver people in the process. If I 'adn't a stopped Cork, the IRA would 'ave got 'old of a lot a gear. I can't say no more cos they made me sign the secrets act as part of lettin' me go."

"So you're a sort of secret agent now?" Suzie asked wide-eyed.

"Nah babe. All I is, is screwed up."

"Never mind Cas, soon you'll just be screwed. Anyway," Suzie pressed. "So yer shot five of them then?"

"Yeah. But it ain't nothin' to be proud of."

"An' it were an old gun?"

"Very old. It were like a cannon. It fair ripped me arms off on the recoil."

"How many times did yer miss Cas?"

"Twice."

"'Ow far away was yer?"

"I dunno. What is this anyway? Twenty fuckin' questions?"

"'Ow far Cas?"

"Forty feet at the most."

"So 'ow comes yer so good? 'Ow comes yer nearly 'it everything yer aimed at? And 'ow comes yer didn't kill no one?"

"Luck?"

"Bollocks!"

"Look Sooze, I couldn't tell no one cos I was sworn to secrecy. Me Uncle Jim taught me 'ow to shoot when I was in me teens. He 'ad an old 'andgun. He told me it were an army service revolver. I used to shoot coconuts off a shy wiv it. I got real good. Uncle Jim said I was a natural. Trouble was he 'ad no licence.

Even so, that piece Cookie 'ad, I say 'ad cos it were confiscated, were a lot bigger an' heavier. Cor, and when it went orf, it were like some bleedin' cannon. It smashed Cork's arm to fuckin' pieces."

"Yer all right now though?"

"Still got a few 'ang ups. Anyway, I'm wearin' a blue skirt. So if I puts on this copper's tunic and add some black stockin's an 'igh 'eels, will that do?"

"I should think so."

"'Ow many do I give yer feller?"

"You'll know. When he really begs yer to stop, or shoots 'is lot, that's the time."

High heels clicking rhythmically on the polished floor, the two women strode with intent toward a cowering Jeff.

"Yer arms achin' are they scumbag?" Suzie demanded.

"Yes milady," he replied in timorous tone.

Released he stood rubbing his cramped limbs. His old soldier as limp as a lettuce leaf, he faced the pair, remembering his place and staring at the floor.

"Yer've bin a bad bugger ain't yer shit 'ead?" Suzie scolded.

"Yes milady."

"What do we do wiv bad buggers eh cretin?" Suzie smiled at Carol explaining with pride. "That's another word what he taught me."

"Them's what yer get in yer soup. Yer knows cretins," Carol corrected.

"Nah. You're thinkin' of croquets. Little 'ard bits that floats in yer soup an' are absolutely tasteless. Yer knows, like you."

"Saucy bitch! Anyways yer's wrong. Croquettes is them tiny spring flowers."

"That's crocuses yer dopey cow!"

"For God's sake!" Jeff cried in despair. "Cretin is an idiot. Croquet is a lawn game. Croquettes are fried things coated with egg and breadcrumbs, croutons are small cubes of toasted or fried bread served with soup and crocus is the spring flower. Crocket, before you get that far, was an American Frontiersman."

Both girls glared, lingering, then said as one. "Shut it arse'ole! That's a cretin." They smirked simultaneously and Carol added. "An' big 'eaded cretins playin' croquet, pickin' crocuses gets rissoled, so watch it!"

Suzie's giggle ignited spontaneously. She shoved Carol, knocking her off balance. Carol retaliated with a swipe of the birch twigs, those stinging the girl's backside.

"Ow! That fuckin' 'urt, yer cow," Suzie cried lunging at the blond. She grabbed her by the blouse, yanking so hard the buttons popped, Carol's cleavage revealed.

Carol paused to view the damage, then growled. "So that's yer game is it?" With the speed of a greyhound out of the traps she had hold of Suzie's maternity smock. The material rent from the shoulders, exposing the surprised girl's breasts, the flesh quivering, tempting. Carol's eyes widened. "Gawd! Look at the size of yer," she squealed.

Suzie held that ruined dress, shocked. Her eyes lifted to see a grinning assailant, hands on hips. "I don't believe yer done that, yer stupid cretin," she snapped.

Springing abruptly, the element of surprise on her side, Suzie caught the blond in a headlock. Her free hand delved between Carol's full breasts, wrenching the cups up and over her bosom.

Jeff watched, transfixed. The proverbial Cheshire cat, his piece reacted, eager to see the next exposure.

Carol, breathing hard; face red; head held tight; fell to the floor, dragging the bigger woman with her. Struggling, a wildcat aroused, she sought the smock again. Hands finding purchase she hauled the garment up, treating Jeff to a glimpse of scant panties, which Carol then desperately tried to relieve Suzie of.

Suzie let go, allowing her captive to crawl away, the exposed mammae gyrating madly with those exertions. Carol, not taking time to compose herself, pounced, seizing the elastic of those briefs.

The challenge was on, who would end up starkers first?

Jeff watched, nursing his torpedo, the idea striking him as being so fine. Little did he realise the fight was spontaneous.

Suzie rolled onto her back, knees drawn up, preventing the underwear, then halfway down her buttocks, from being removed completely. Carol straddled her, back to the clawing brunette. She leant over the bump and continued to haul on those white pants, impervious to the nails raking her back.

Suzie, jaw set, caught hold of the blonde's jacket and tore it complete with blouse from her shoulders. No sooner had the clothing gone and Carol's arms been released, did she continue her frenzied actions. Not happy until she had finally torn the panties from Suzie's ankles.

The blond vixen spun around, hurling her trophy at Jeff, and began working on the remains of Suzie's ripped dress. The pregnant woman would have none of it. She clawed at her assailant's tresses, managing to pull her to the floor.

Rolling, she released Carol effectively throwing her clear, and as the blond struggled to gain her feet, Suzie grabbed hold of the girl's waistband. Skirt, panties, suspender and stockings slid ungracefully to her ankles.

Carol tripped on the tangle, falling flat, providing Jeff with a bird's eye view of her tremulous rump. With a twist of her body, Suzie managed to relieve Carol of it all, the blond flailing, only her brassiere left, hiding nothing.

The brunette too slow in her assault on that final strip of clothing, permitted a near naked Carol to pounce, to peel the torn smock from her back and arms, not desisting until she had stripped the thrashing limbs and Suzie lay bereft of all clothing.

Carol climbed slowly to her feet. Panting, hands on hips, she stared down at the defeated opponent. "I.......won," she gasped.

Suzie offered her a hand. "'Elp a distressed pregnant damsel get up," she pleaded.

Carol obliged, complaining. "Gawd, yer weighs a ton."

Suzie rested her head on Carol's shoulder, her arms encircling the girl's waist. Her hands ascended and surreptitiously unfastened the brassiere. Then straightening whisked it off, crying. "An' I come second."

The pair stared at one another, breathless. Jeff gazed in awe at both, his own lungs labouring. Suzie tentatively stroked Carol's breast, the blond smiled.

Suzie's hand swept away the flaxen mane, fingers caressing the nape of her neck, she eased her friend's, lover's head forward, meeting her half way with parted lips. They kissed, Carol embracing her with roaming hands. She provoked. Suzie reciprocated, intimate parts tenderly touched.

Their mouths held suspended in rapturous courtship, smooching, manipulating; lush velvet to luxurious satin. Full lips searched bountiful offering. Tongues delved, dancing simultaneously. Naked bodies entwined, breast to breast, groin to groin.

Jeff was in a spin. Wow! predominated. What seventy percent of men wish to witness was paraded before him. A pure mind bending act of lesbianism.

They were two young lovers expressing their feelings in physical passion. Two young women tenderly exploring one another's substance. To love another with the mind and to express that verbally is construed as caring. To love physically, an extension of the oral declaration is taboo, unless socially acceptable or fashionable.

Mouth to mouth, oblivious to their witness, insensible to the world, concerned only for the immediate clinch, the women explored. Hands stroked warm inviting flesh. Carol's descended her intimate's back to fall upon and fondle the fullness of her buttocks; that other hand kept Suzie pressed to her, bosom cushioned to bosom, nipples aroused and erect.

It was Carol that broke that emphatic embrace, to fall to Suzie's breast, pecking, licking and suckling the long teat; her partner panting, sighing with those exacting attentions. The brunette titillated, Carol descended ever downward, over the distended abdomen and beneath. She teased the groin, tongue flicking between slim thighs, aggravating the wanton slit.

Carol traversed the hip, tending the succulent loins, again kissing and caressing. Her hand passed between the olive thighs to stimulate the irritated. Fingers gently probed the soft labia, the mouth continuing with its excitement of the curvaceous cheeks.

The blond dipped a digit, the pussy lips spreading, the insertion delving, searching, probing. Her tongue slid deliberately down the buttock cleft, to lick erotically about the investigative finger. Suzie, eyes closed, moaned, the pleasantries exciting, the edge of paradise so close, her lust overwhelming.

Two fingers, then three toyed with her tightness, the thumb massaging the sexual centre, the tongue then tantalising the anus.

Rising, withdrawing from the vaginal juice, Carol's arms cuddled from behind, fondling Suzie's breasts, the firm orbs swollen by pregnancy filling her hands, the teats ultra sensitive.

One hand fell to the groin, a nail tracing a path to the tight curled mons, while a wet tongue teased Suzie's swan like neck and delicate ear; Carol relishing the girl's resulting shivers.

Suzie gasped. "Gawd Cas! Yer knows what yer doin' all right. I'd forgotten 'ow good yer was. Shit face." Jeff was snapped from his own deliberations, his hand flew from the stiff poker he stroked. "I 'opes yer takin' notes."

Jeff needed no such instruction. "I am. I am," he quickly assured her.

Carol took to the floor, taking her unresisting lover with her. The blond seductress lay on her back, her legs wide. Suzie knelt astride the girl's face, bottom thrust up, Carol's wet orifice anticipating a warm probe. The brunette descended to that glistening mons, hopeful of reciprocation.

Suzie was not to be disappointed. Whilst she bent to her particular invasion, Carol's legs rising to accommodate, heels tucked to Suzie's shoulders, the blond feverishly set to her own singular lust. The thumb of one hand toyed with Suzie's arsehole, while the other played havoc with her clitoris. To add to the euphoria Carol's tongue glided deliciously within the vaginal folds, electrifying that organ.

Suzie similarly stimulated, licking sweetly about the blond's nub. Jeff, beyond himself, played continuously with his ramrod, the itch unbearable. He listened enthralled, to the sounds of passion emanating from the naked clinch that lay on the floor before him.

Suspending preliminaries, her tongue and jaw aching, Carol asked quietly, her chin dripping with the mix of saliva and vaginal mucus. "Jeff. 'Ave yer any rubbers?"

Shaken from his solicitudes, he stammered. "Y....Yeah. Yeah sure." Grabbing one from a drawer he handed the foil to Carol.

"No Jeff," she said. "Put it on. Better still get it out an' slip it over the end of yer dick." Jeff complied happily.

Carol gripped the base of that shaft and pulled the capped dome to her open mouth. Carefully she guided the roll on with her teeth, drawing him into her. Jeff's cock ached with the impossible angle, his attitude intense with the slow immersion. Carol's lips tightened about his circumference. Her tongue stroked his crown, her fingers fondling his balls.

Releasing him, much too his disappointment, Carol held Suzie's cheeks apart. "Give yer good lady a sound rogerin'," she said.

Jeff held back, objecting. "But Sooze doesn't like it that way."

"That's cos you ain't bin doin' it right mate. Get us a dildo. Nothin' too big. Six inches'll do."

Jeff returned promptly with a latex stiff. Suzie still tended Carol's privates, the sensations intense.

Carol held the creamy cheeks apart once more. "Go on Jeff. But only yer 'ead. Don't put it all in, not yet."

Suzie grunted as her anus was stretched, whether in pain or delight was not clear. Carol simultaneously gave her a twist of the latex dick. To Suzie's continuous guttural expletives Carol led Jeff in by his balls. Carol worked her, the latex servicing her cunt while the McCoy plumbed her arse.

Suzie squirmed. She abandoned the dutiful pussy lick and pushed up on all fours, her sweet countenance a picture of intense concentration. Her features tensed as the play brought her close. Carol maintained Jeff's steady pace, his part only intended to heighten the excitement, the dildo kindling the climax. Carol wanted the lad's seed retained, he had other duties to fulfil, she didn't want him disinterested.

Suzie shuddered, squealing. "Jesus H. Christ! Fuckin' 'ell! What a screw!" Rolling on her back the dildo and Jeff springing free, she lay panting, her thighs squeezed together, knees drawn up. "Bestest fuck ever!" she declared. Jeff looked away, taking the comment as yet another put down.

"Come on Jeff," Carol cajoled. "Get another rubber on."

Jeff placed another over the end of his rigid piece and glanced at Carol expectantly.

"Yer wants me to put it on again?" she teased. Jeff nodded, the eager beaver. Carol gripped his hard meat and standing, her eyes on his, slid the rubber over his length, prolonging the pleasure by stroking out all the creases. Fingers firmly holding him, she squeezed the thin film as she repeatedly pushed back to his groin, Jeff's buttocks flexing with each and every delightful sensation.

"Don't want it coming off do we big boy?" Carol mewed, Jeff unable to comment.

Her expression, was one of endearment as she curled an arm about Jeff's neck and drew him to her waiting mouth. Warm sensuous lips embraced him; her kiss a touch of paradise. Her hot breath sweet as spring's blue belled copse.

She held him, his hand to her breast. He fondled gladly, the soft flesh filling his hand, his thumb caressing the hard teat.

"Fancy me?" Carol asked, her voice a whisper.

Jeff cast a glance at his recumbent intended.

"Don't worry about what Sooze might think. D'yer fancy me?"

"You're breathtaking," he replied so quietly she could barely hear him.

"Yer makes me sound like a view from Blackpool Tower."

"You're paradise found," Jeff added.

"It's getting' better. Paradise eh? If I'm paradise what would yer call that tight wet 'ole between me legs? The one that is achin' for that long thick prick of yours."

"How about the cavern of bliss?"

"That's good. Yeah ain't bad at all. Now me tits, what of them?" Their voices were mere murmurs, words for each other's ears only.

"Suckler's heaven set upon silken dunes."

"Yer good at this ain't yer boy? Me arse Jeff. Describe me arse."

"A seductive gorge set in snowy hills."

"Is it? Seductive?"

"I'd like to plant a stem there," Jeff answered.

"Yer dirty minded bugger! Legs. What's my legs like?"

"Sun kissed limbs of Aphrodite."

"Yer've done this before, ain't yer sweet talker?"

"No, but it is easy with such explicit beauty."

"I've run out of bits now," Carol moaned.

"Eyes," Jeff persevered. "Liquid pools of ice, fired by the passion of seduction. Lips, soft petals of the wild rose. Skin, sweet as nectar, smooth as silk, warm and inviting like a mid winter's log fire. Oh sweet dream, to nestle my fortunate body close to yours."

"Now yer is getting' carried away. Jeff yer can carry me away, to that leather couch thingy over there. Spread me legs and plant yer marrow. Fuck me Jeff. Don't spare the horses."

He scooped her up in his strong arms and carried her effortlessly to the padded leather. An apparatus for face down or face up chastisement, depending on the fancy. He lay her down, she drawing her legs up, the supple limbs easily coping with the contortion, as she tucked her knees to her breasts. Provocatively she traced a finger about her anus.

Jeff needed no more hints, placing his piece to the puckered hole he slid in, the orifice giving grudgingly to his intrusion. Carol indulged her pleasure centre, massaging the bubble of wonder.

He rode her with an ardour, content to shaft, she stimulated by his actions.

"Don't yer come yet," Carol warned. "I want that dick kept stiff."

Jeff fucked her steadily, not daring to off load his seed, continuing until his withdrawal was indicated.

Carol rolled from the couch, landing on her feet, then bent over the seat her legs wide. Jeff discarding the rubber sank into her offered depths, she so wet he could barely feel the connection.

Body taut with concentration he withdrew, thrusting back in with force, his groin smacking against her buttocks.

"That's it Jeff, give us it all!" Carol urged. "Fuck me drippin' wet cunt wiv all yer got. Shove it in 'ard. Let me feel yer go up me. Give us yer rock 'ard prick. Faster. Faster Jeff."

Jeff tried to please, his cock lunging in and out, pumping her, the orifice sucking to each withdrawal such was her exudation. That body jarred to each thrust, pendulous breasts swinging with the force of his entries.

"Ooh that's so good," Carol mumbled to herself.

"Suzie," she suddenly shouted. "Get orf yer fat arse an' come 'ere."

"Cheeky fuckin' cow!" Suzie retorted, demanding angrily. "Who d'yer think yer talkin' to?"

"Not a fuckin' milady that's for sure."

"What yer want anyway? An' d'yer realise yer got me common law right up inside yer? Thievin' bitch!"

"An' real nice he is too."

The verbal discourse was sustained without interruption to the sexual intercourse, the girls impervious to Jeff's deliberations.

"Now give me tits a squeeze gel," Carol invited rather than demanded, her own hands grasped Suzie's, who in turn stooped to return the stimulation.

"Don't burn 'im out Cas. I will need 'im again sometime yer knows."

"Uh! Uh!" Carol replied, tensing to the young man's sudden increased ardour.

"Oh Jeff, go on 'arder," Carol goaded. "Fuck me 'arder."

Her naked form shuddered with each increased thrust. "Go on boy right up, force it right up. Give us yer stiff. I want it all. Let me feel yer slap against me arse," she urged, her face contorted with the pleasures of his plunging, stuffing actions.

"Oh! That's it. That's it!" she squealed. "I wants yer come. I wants it all. I wanna feel that sticky seed, yer hot spunk pumpin' inside me," she raged.

"Cream me cunt Jeff. Give us the lot," Carol cried, her voice hoarse.

"Screw me!" She sucked air; blond strands adhered to her damp skin.

"Fuck me! Faster!" she yelled.

"Harder! Fuck me! Screw me!" the blond screamed, face wet with perspiration, eyes clamped tightly shut in concentration.

"Harder Jeff. Harder boy." Her teeth clenched and back arched as Jeff's efforts bore fruit. A scowl appeared, the eyebrows knitting. "Uh! Uh! Uh! Uh! Uh! Uh!" she grunted to each powerful thrust, her fingers painfully digging the meat of Suzie's breasts.

Hands about Carol's hips, digits burrowing the flesh, Jeff hammered like a steam engine at full bore, her succulence bringing him ever-nearer orgasm.

Carol sucked air more rapidly, her sharp, deep intakes more profound, rasping noisily, a guttural squeal to each. Jeff persisted, his own breathing laboured, his body also glistening with the moisture of exertion, the sensation below dangerously close. He struggled desperately to keep his seed contained.

Suzie's bosom released, Carol lifted her torso clear of the padded leather, her spine curved, bottom nicely pronounced, the flesh quivering to the noisy slaps from Jeff's groin. A sigh escaped her changing to a hum, that rapidly developed into a high pitched roar. Carol's arms grabbed Suzie, pulling her close, those limbs hugging, her talons scratching, clawing Suzie's back.

"Ram it in. I'm there. I'm there. For fuck's sake ram it in. Slap my arse and shove the mother fucker in." A final breathless, foul-mouthed demand from Carol indicated the proximity of her climax. The request happily met by a tiring Jeff. His palm punished her haunches in her final throws of orgasm, Jeff's seed pumping between her legs as the embers in her backside faded.

With Carol in her arms, Suzie remarked. "Still quiet I see."

36

Figure Chapter 5 When Needs Must

4-When Needs Must

Cork lit a cigarette, a habit he had despised until his incarceration. Long hours spent in self-inflicted solitude, he had finally succumbed. Boredom had gripped his intellect in a vice. Smoking had eased the frustration. Drugs would have been better he had often thought, but he had needed to remain in control.

It was too late to go visiting. Anyway there was another need that required satisfying. A thirst generated from eight months inside that had to be quenched.

Turning up his jacket collar, the lapels pinched together in an attempt to keep out the bitter chill, Cork sought a taxi. Half midnight and a half dozen cabs ranked outside Waterloo Station waiting on fares.

The first in the line offered a warm refuge from the icy night air, that comfort meeting him as he opened a rear door. Climbing in, a shiver snatching the words from him, he stammered. "K....Kings C......Cross." Before he could add the address a sneeze heralded its imminence cutting him short.

"Where abouts in Kings Cross Guv?" the driver inquired not bothering to look around.

"The." Cork sneezed. "Station," he quickly added, sniffing back the sudden rush. Hands impatiently searched pockets seeking a wipe. There were none. Damn! Cork considered the sleeve. Perhaps not, the jacket may have to last him for some time. He sniffed harder.

"Cold?" the bulldog faced driver asked.

"Fucking freezing," Cork replied, deliberately misunderstanding.

Cork was rewarded by an increase in temperature; the blowers turned on full. The driver said no more, much to Cork's relief.

The City, chaotic, noisy and dirty by day seemed eerie by night. Still dirty, but not so obviously so. There were late revellers about. Occasional cars raced the odd hundred yards between endless traffic lights. But the after midnight metropolis was a far cry from the congested hubbub of the waking London.

Stars fought to be seen through a lazy hazy curtain of mixed pollutants. The reflection in the Thames a shimmering confusion of city lights, Waterloo Bridge itself devoid of tomorrow's recycled metals.

The taxi's diesel purred across the Strand, along Aldwych before turning into Kingsway, the two miles soon traversed. Cork wordless, settled his fare and strode off into the night.

Years had passed by since he had last sought solace in that neighbourhood. Time hadn't altered the scarred townscape though. The old railway bridge needed a coat of paint where whores, even at that time of night, paraded their wares.

"'Ello luvvy. Want a good time?" a coarse chesty voice assailed him. The owner a busty peroxided blond. Cork summed her up. Ageing. Past her sell by date. Those years having been very unkind, that is if she ever had anything worth offering in the first place. He shook his head and moved on. There were plenty to choose from.

Approached a half dozen times, all hopefuls repelled by a shake of the head, a possibility final stepped from the shadows. Dark haired and eyed, the prostitute, slim of figure appealed.

"What do you do?" Cork asked, his exhaustion evident.

She was young, just what he desired. "What would you like?" she replied, her voice soft and sensuous.

"Tell me, do you possess the requisite tools for a certain discomfiture of the lower regions?" he inquired, avoiding precision, knowing that if she did she would understand.

"I cater for all persuasions," she answered, winking.

"A tart with a command of the English language, how refreshing," Cork applauded in his own inimical manner.

"Is that a back-handed compliment sailor?" She smiled, her eyes sparkling.

"I speak only the truth. No lies. Do you have a base we can play in?"

"Five minutes walk, unless you have a motor."

"Nothing up my sleeve. Let's walk."

Sandra's abode was cramped but clean. She seemed to take a pride in her flat as well as her looks. Under the improved lighting Cork was surprised at how attractive she really was. He knew if she had a mind to, she could go places. Climb the ladder of sexual servitude.

Large ebony eyes, highlighted in emerald, assessed Cork. Those jet chips set in a pleasant narrow face, the nose dainty, her full lips painted green to complement the sparkling gems, which so effortlessly held Cork transfixed. Rouge filled her hollow cheeks, a striking camouflage.

Her body slim, she sported a delicate bust partially exposed by a deep cut, tight fitting black lycra top.

A short tight skirt displayed the length and shapeliness of her seductive black stocking clad legs; her bottom stretching that skirt demonstrating what treats lay within.

"Coffee?" she offered.

"I could do with warming," Cork confessed.

"Yes, but coffee first?" she joked smiling, the bait of a temptress.

"Warm the inside, then the outside later," Cork unnecessarily clarified.

Hot Expresso before them, Sandra probed. "So have you any speciality in mind?"

"Have you any apparatus?" Cork countered.

"Very limited," she admitted. "Though if you are also into bondage, I could tie you over the back of a chair and tan your bare arse," she suggested.

Cork replaced the steaming coffee cup, his face serious. "I do believe we have a misunderstanding miss."

"Oh!" Sandra stared puzzled.

"It is **your** hide **I** wish to tan."

"Oh no, I'm sorry. I'm not into pain. I always do the whipping," she said determined.

"Excellent! Beating someone who enjoys it seems so pointless. But think dear girl it will be an invaluable experience. Open up new avenues. You will then appreciate what your clients want. You will have been there. Know what is required. Have no fear I shall tread carefully. Believe me, applied by an experienced hand, a caning can be most erotic."

"You can bullshit all you like mister. If I do it at all, I'll do it for money. So do you have the readies?"

"How much?"

"Two hundred."

"You don't come cheap," Cork remarked taking his roll from a jacket pocket. "Do you possess a cane?"

Sandra shivered. There was something about Cork that upset her. The thought of a rod slashing her backside didn't help either. Caned at a private girls only school had hurt her considerably. She had never forgotten that painful experience. But she desperately needed money. Business was slack, the rent and her pimp were due.

She conceded, perhaps too readily. "A round dozen and that it is," she told Cork adamant. "I have other clients to think of."

"Fair enough." He drained his coffee cup. "Where?" he asked impatient.

"Next door. The spare room."

Sandra led the way, Cork savouring the roll of her hips, those full cheeks pressing delightfully against the tight skirt. *'It's been too long,'* he acknowledged.

The tart placed his money under a clock on the mantle piece and opened the door to the room in question.

Sandra Allcock, nineteen, had not been on the game very long. Still naïve, there had been no bad experiences, not yet. Most of the clientele visited and paid for a quick fuck. The local entrenched whores had been unusually kind, accommodating even, accepting the novice onto their territory.

She picked up most nights, but was not doing the trade she needed, hence her acceptance of Cork's custom even though the man frightened her.

Born of good stock, Sandra had tired of the boring life laid down by her pious, overbearing parents. One night six months before, she had slipped away in the night to the bright lights.

Approached by a pimp, a seemingly charming Turk, she found herself beguiled by the easy money to be made by a pretty girl.

That young Muslim had turned her head; alternatively sleeping with her and renting her out, first to specific friends, and then all and sundry. He held her in thrall, initially with infatuation and then by a savage streak.

The first men had been repugnant, but the life became easier, she had quickly degenerated, accepting, if not indulging in her forced vocation. The Turk only visited now for money or sex.

Nervous, of Cork and for her arse, Sandra placed a high-backed chair in the middle of the room. From a cupboard she took several coils of rope and a long rattan, complete with crook.

"Only twelve," she reminded.

"Of course," Cork readily agreed.

"Shall I take my clothes off?" she asked.

With deliberately false severity Cork informed her. "There is only one way to chastise a naughty girl." He paused smiling, the eyes cold, unfeeling. "On the bare backside."

He was turning her on. Why? How? That didn't happen very often with a client, many's the time a dab of KY had saved the day.

"Of course sir," she agreed. "Shall I slip them off, or will you do it?"

Cork sat on a chair toying with the cane. "**You** strip. Slowly if you please. I haven't seen a woman in a long time."

Sandra commenced an intoxicating expose. Boots placed to one side, she lifted a stockinged foot to his groin, her toes stirring the sleeping worm. With an alluring smile, not returned by the stony faced Cork, she soothed the skirt up, revealing the nylon's top and the pale flesh beyond.

There in the shadow, the vee of her white nylon briefs framed the auburn coils of her mound, clearly visible through the intricate lace. Cork stared impassive.

Teasing, she rolled the stocking, exposing the soft thigh. She stooped, her face inches from his cold bearing, her eyes seeking his soul. The stocking removed she draped it over his shoulder as a final touch. The partner soon followed suit.

Turning her back, her mind disturbed by the man's lack of emotion, she raised the skirt, slowly revealing voluptuous round buttocks, naked but for a 'G' string tight in the cleft of her butt.

She spun to face him, peeling the skimpy top upwards, revealing a white lacy brassiere. The top she tossed to him, Cork dodging it, allowing the richly perfumed garment to fall to the floor.

Sandra unclipped the bra, the catch in front, and with seduction in mind, eased the cups apart. Her breasts, larger than Cork expected, bounced free, nipples set high, erect, the encircling pink virginal.

She advanced on Cork. Paused before him legs spread, the minimal 'v' of her panties disappearing between the soft lips of her pussy.

Invited, Cork slid a hand beneath the cloth and fingered her sex. She leant to him, breasts swaying enticing before his face. He kissed one, then the other.

She drifted away, stopping at the back of a chair. Cork rose. She bent over, the man removing her pants. Naked she presented her backside for his dubious pleasures. Cork collected up the ropes.

He positioned her arms behind her back and bound the wrists tightly. The bond was then passed about her waist and retied to her wrists, thus securing her hands above the buttock flesh.

Cork roped her elbows, pulling them toward each other, until the arms resisted any further pressure, the bosom thrust tantalising. Ankles were dealt with next, lashed to the individual chair legs. Her thighs were tended similarly purely for good measure.

A tether was then placed to enhance her discomfort, about her chest, above and below the breasts. Those two ropes were drawn together, knotted in her cleavage, the coarse fibres biting into the supple mounds.

Cork then vindictively added a further two ligatures to either side of those breasts, fixed to the top and bottom nylon twists. Those he passed beneath the chair and around the rear cross member, drawing the girl into a bending position. He tied the ropes off.

He selected the stockings and smiling to himself, rolled one into a ball. That he stuffed into Sandra's mouth. The second nylon he looped about her jaw and nape several times. He knotted the stocking, ensuring it was tight, not happy until the nylon bit into the corners of her mouth, separating her teeth. She was then effectively gagged.

Cane in hand Cork studied her proffered cheeks, the flesh so stretched he could see her anus.

Incapable of movement, let alone avoidance, Sandra began to fret. Already her position was uncomfortable, the slightest movement upward increased the cut on her bosom. Should she react in that way to the caning, she would garrotte her bust. She feared for herself albeit with good reason.

Cork tapped her pale cheeks lightly, gauging the swing, mentally preparing for the delivery.

"For what you are about to receive," he whispered. "May I be truly thankful."

Sandra tensed, dread consuming her. She knew the caning must smart, she couldn't however, anticipate by how much.

The rod withdrew to shoulder height. A hiss denoted its downward arc. The deft flick of a wrist to enhance the strike and the solid implement sliced her lower buttocks, curving to her shape. An almighty swack resounded about the room.

Sandra couldn't scream, the gag proficient in her silence. Instead a muffled growl climbed her throat, as a biting scorch ripped through her nether region. Her eyes flung wide with shock she chewed the nylon gag. Tears rapidly welled as she succumbed to the awful pain, wishing then she had never undertaken Cork's request.

That fire in her arse still proved beyond reason as she heard the vile weapon cut air again. Barely aware of the sonorous report as the cane ripped into her backside, Sandra was otherwise overwhelmed by the monumental hurt that surged through her rear.

She tried desperately, hopelessly, to pull free from her bonds, those ligatures as planned, cutting deep into her breasts. She fell back into place, knowing escape impossible.

Cork aware of her agonised writhing and enjoying every sick second of her pronounced suffering, prepared another detonation.

The rod swished, connecting violently mid-butt, Sandra's skin so tight and there no meat to absorb the stroke, the breath was driven from her.

Again Sandra attempted to rise, that impact so relentless, but again the ropes cut those tender breasts.

Unyielding buttocks shuddered to the return of the irresistible rattan, her face contorted about the gag, her tears spilled in tribulation. It was too much. The bastard was an absolute fiend. If only she had known.

Three thick purpling welts adorned her hide, a fourth flourished, her backside kissed by the sun.

The fifth visited with dreadful power the scant flesh atop the buttocks, immediately below the bound hands; a downward slash, forceful in its extreme. That cut reminiscent of being branded.

Another Cork laid alongside, doubling the effect. The whore twisted and squirmed. Snot flowed, converging with the flood of tears soaking her gag, auburn hair adhering annoyingly to her wet face. Never, ever, would she succumb to that again. Never would she allow another to take such advantage again. Sandra had learned a difficult lesson. There would always be those like Cork.

He dealt her a rigorous cut to her thighs. If Sandra had considered the pain thus far extreme, she then discovered it could get worse.

Smirking, Cork located the crease below her cheeks with an unsparing corker. Gleefully he noted her muffled squeal, so dealt her a duplicate. Her torso twisted with the crucifixion, the smart smouldering on.

Her body sticky from pain and struggling, the ropes abrading her sensitive skin, she received the ninth welter, the small plump area at the base of her arse cavorting to its impact. Slowly the ladder formed, angry stripes lay one above the other, her whole derriere singing the song of suffering.

Down the rattan slammed. No let up. The now familiar hard smack as the vine welted that previously untainted flesh, indenting, despatching waves of scalding agony through her battered hide.

Only two to go. Sandra thanked God. Nearly over. She wouldn't sit for a week if she was lucky. She would claw his eyes out when released, the bastard.

He revisited her thighs, whipping them high up, before the complete separation. She couldn't take any more. Thank God it was nearly over.

The final sadistic slice cannoned in, mid cheeks. A flood of fire coated her behind. She let her tensions burst, believing it finished.

Cork put down his cane and untied an ankle. At last! Sandra waited for revenge, her bottom continuing to sting with a vengeance. Then much to her anguish he forced her foot to the other side of the chair leg and re-secured it, doing the same with her other ankle.

No! Her fears were soon ratified. He had spread her further, tightening the already taut bottom. Cork released the ropes to her chest, then yanked her down until her breasts cushioned on the seat.

He can't! No! Not more?

Cork mauled the hot flesh, running his fingers over the crimson butt, smoothing the fiery welts. Sandra was aware of him then walking away. She contorted, trying to see. He was in her cupboard, bent, searching. He sprung up, his hands filled.

"You have been holding out on me you filthy whore! See what you have been hiding." Jubilantly he held up a wickedly thick cane, dark brown in colour. In his other hand he grasped a wide strap, twin tailed and painfully thick. "Now we can get down to some serious flogging," he informed her solemnly. Sandra came close to passing out, then and there.

"Once I have flayed your hide with this strap you will understand real suffering. Especially when I beat you with the cane again," Cork grimly promised.

'Why?' She wanted to scream. 'Why?'

Because I want to, he would have replied.

That strap hurt, stung beyond belief. The twin tails assailed the welts raised by the cane. Sandra glistened. Sweat beads pooled. Formed tiny rivulets. Ran up her back. Trickled between the scarlet blistered cheeks. Soaked her cleavage and wet her thighs. Her lithe body constantly tensed, was rigid with the blinding pain. The ropes mauled her, bruising where they cut her struggling torso.

A dozen or so times that strap cracked down, whipping her buttocks to a frenzy, a whirlpool of abject misery. Not content with administering that, he flailed her inner thighs, the tongues ravishing the silky soft tissue. That sting terrifying.

He ceased, sweating profusely. Then Cork selected that awful cane and flexed it between sticky palms. Sandra sensed the cool touch. She clenched her teeth, anticipating its vile impact. She wasn't disappointed. When that dark fibrous rod struck, it carried her to hell, an insight to Dante's Inferno. It was too much. She felt her senses deserting her. A delightful pool of dark loomed, but the slap of another stroke wrenched her back to purgatory.

Cork dealt her six strokes, breaking the skin in several places. He sighed, temporarily fulfilled and threw the rod to one side. Loosing his tool and with no thought or precaution thrust it into the girl's backside. A new pain! Sharp teeth tearing at her anus.

Cork aroused by her battered behind, heightened that excitement with his insertion. He had a preference for seeing his prick securely grasped, and it was, the hole stretched to his circumference. He studied his movements. The stiff glided in and out, heedless of Sandra's discomfiture.

His pace quickened. He slapped against her at a steady pace. Each thrust forceful, not happy until his groin met with her hot cheeks. He withdrew until the head was nearly out and then launched back in, finally shooting his milky sperm deep within her rectum.

Without so much as a thank you for your arse, let alone releasing the beaten wretch, Cork zipped up his piece and opened the door to the sitting room. He stopped dead in his tracks for there relaxed in an armchair sat the Turkish pimp.

"Have a good time my friend?" the Eurasian asked, flashing gold through his smile.

"None of your fucking business chummy! And I'm not your friend and never likely to be slime ball," Cork snapped.

The man merely laughed. "Where is Sandra? Getting dressed?"

"Look for yourself," Cork suggested.

"I'll wait," he said.

Cork lifted the time piece and retrieved his two hundred.

"What are you doing?" the Turk demanded.

"I'm not satisfied with the service. So I'm refunding my money." Cork pocketed the wad.

"I don't think so my friend." The young man rose. About the same height and build as Cork he had the edge provided by youth. Cork simply smiled, disarming.

The Turk was at him. A flick knife deftly produced from a pocket, the blade sprang to Cork's throat. From that position Sandra's bound naked body could be seen. The young man frowned. "What have you.........?"

That moments relaxation was all Cork needed. With his revolver barrel jammed under the pimp's jaw he remarked. "Nice suit. I wish I had one like that. Drop the knife cunt, or I'll spread your empty skull over the ceiling." The knife clattered to the floor.

"Now you fucking wog, let's go see the girlfriend." As the Turk turned away Cork struck him hard on the back of the head; the man stumbled forward, Cork assisting his progress with a kick in the behind. "A reminder cunt! Don't fuck with me again. Now strip!"

The pimp had no doubts about Cork, one hundred percent bastard. So he removed his clothing, stopping at the boxer shorts. He waited bewildered for further instruction.

"I said strip, you thick prick. I can see that I am going to have to teach you a severe lesson," he barked. The boxer shorts rapidly descended.

Cork threw him a rope. "Tie that around your left wrist. Tight mind you." He watched amused as the young man nervously complied. "Now that thing between your legs. I want it up and running. Play with it man, its going places." The familiar vindictive smirk played on his lips.

The Eurasian embarrassed fondled himself. "Per'aps," he suggested. "If you pointed that gun elsewhere I might manage it."

Cork's grin widened. "Worry you does it? So it should. However I wouldn't want you to think that I'm not serious. If you've a problem demonstrating your manhood look away. Might I suggest you run your eye over your floozy. Her backside is of particular interest at the moment. Don't get too jealous will you, because I can assure you there is no need."

Gradually the pecker expanded. Continuous manipulation before a bemused tyrant finally had an effect. The man stood proud.

Cork laughed. "Big fellow aren't you coon? Lay over your tart's back, your prick up her arse." He watched him, aware of Sandra's grunt as the thick cock penetrated. "Treat for you eh? Like a bit of arse do you?"

Warily Cork rounded the pair, the mouth of the gun barrel never pointing away from the Turk. "Put your arms around her chest."

Kneeling Cork placed the revolver in the hand of his seemingly disabled arm. Lifting that limb he pushed the gun to the man's testicles, then he released the rope holding her down, retying it as she came horizontal.

He leant forward, the gun remaining in pace and looped the rope from the Turk's wrist about one of Sandra's already bound breasts. He tightened it, looped it about its twin and secured the man's free hand there.

"There mother fucker you can have a grope. Beware though. You pull on your hands and you'll cut her tits off." He laughed, pleased with his efforts, adding. "You look lovely. Shit in harmony. Still you've both company in your long hours of waiting."

He gagged the scowling Eurasian with his own boxer shorts, tearing them to suit. Then as a finishing touch bound the man's ankles to Sandra's and added a rope about their waists.

"Incidentally," Cork said thoughtful. "I enjoy a bit of arse hole myself. In fact I was up her just before you. Your dick me old mate is soaking in my seed. If that doesn't worry you then perhaps the fact I have Syphilis might. If you ever get loose, I should see a Doc."

Cork picked up the thick cane and slashed the olive buttocks, the Turk jumping with the sudden shock, his hands automatically tightening the loops about Sandra's breasts, those suffering severe friction burns.

A dozen he dealt, with all the force he could muster. The buttocks danced wildly to the rod's violence, the young man yelping with each delivery. Much as he tried to keep his hands still it was impossible. The pain inflicted caused him time and again to forget. By the cessation of hostilities and Cork's exercise in retribution, the pimp's backside was black and blue.

Cork tossed the rattan to one side telling the pair. "Enjoy each other. I'll maybe ring the police later and let them know you are here, and there again I might not. Have fun." There he left them, lover's entwined.

Cork stepped out onto the street, garbed in an expensive Armani two piece, his wallet full and the keys to a Jaguar automatic in his hand.

48

Figure Chapter 5 Bath Time

5-Bath Time

Dawn heralded a cold damp misty day in deepest, darkest Cornwall. Jeff cooked breakfast, his heavily pregnant woman still in the throes of craving.

"Bacon and ice cream. Ugh!" he moaned.

That wasn't all he had to complain about. Due to the girl's spontaneous orgy the night before, he had missed his whipping. Now he was being made to suffer.

Suzanne thought it hilarious. Carol sniggered continuously. In fact every time they caught sight of Jeff they collapsed in hysterics.

The poor bastard had been ordered to don the maid's uniform. He stumbled about in high heels, garbed in a short black dress with white laced bib and collar. He wore the black stockings of the appointment, held up by suspenders.

The devious calculating duo had also outfitted him with frilly brassiere and crotchless panties, so his privates hung from the opening. Not content with just the uniform they had, giggling like schoolgirls, plastered his face in make-up.

Every time he had cause to come close, hands ventured up his skirt to pinch his bum or grope his tackle. Humiliated he was. Excited he was. Looking forward to the spanking he had been promised from both, he was. Poor misguided fool.

First he had to cook breakfast. Then he had to bath them both. Suzie had declared that on completion of those two tasks, (Well one task and one pleasure), he would receive a sound spanking from Carol to the duration of an egg timer. 'To be sure he's done' Suzie had said.

That completed, Suzie would continue the flagellation for another three minutes, and then Jeff would suffer them both simultaneously raiding his buttocks for another run of the egg timer. Each time the lad contemplated the promise, his skirt exhibited a certain bulge.

One deliciously greasy fry-up. Carol wolfed the lot. Suzie examined her plate and pushed it away. "Seemed like a good idea at the time," she affirmed, feeling sick.

"'Ow can bacon an' ice cream ever be a good idea?" Carol asked, sliding her hand up Jeff's thigh, he stationed beside her. His firm expression melted as fingers toyed with his nuts. "D'yer know I could play wiv them all day," she said.

"Feel free," Jeff whispered under the heavenly influence.

Scowling, Suzie threw a verbal spanner into his works. "Did I say you could speak?" she demanded.

Jeff quickly responded with. "Sorry milady."

"Yer will be!" Suzie barked, once again cogitating on breakfast. She cut a piece of bacon, dipped it in the melting ice cream and forked it into her mouth. An expression of pure bliss soothed the frown.

"Yer sick!" Carol gasped, wrinkling her nose.

"Zac wants. Zac gets," Suzie retorted.

"I just 'opes Zac ain't 'is father's son. A real lady man eh?" Carol gibed, giggling.

"Nah!" Suzie shook her head. "Zac's got a spine. The scan showed that up."

Jeff stormed out, shouting back in a petulant tone. "He's got a brain as well, so he won't take after his mother."

Suzie smouldered. She glared at the retreating scivvy. "Seems he's not as well trained as he should be. I'll put that right later on."

"Yer shouldn't keep on at 'im like that Sooze. He'll get a complex." Carol cautioned rising from her seat.

"Are yer takin' the piss or what? Get a complex? For fuck's sake he's got one as big as the Eiffel! Or ain't yer noticed?"

"Then 'elp 'im."

"I do," Suzie protested. "I gives 'im what he wants."

"Yer means twisted sex. Perverted sex. Sex. Sex an' sex."

"Yeah, what else?"

"Love an' understandin'?"

Suzie inspected her cuticles. "That's the trouble gel, I don't."

"Then why stay? Why string the poor bugger along?"

"I've got 'is bun ain't I?"

"An' he's got the dosh. Yer tart."

"He's 'appy."

"Nah he ain't. He's 'opin', that's what he is."

"What should I do then? Go on the social, some poxy flat. Bring up Zac on tuppence a week? Jeff don't want that."

"I don't know. But I knows yer won't be 'appy, not like this."

"We'll see."

An hour later the three were larking about in the bathroom. Jeff had been kneeling by the sunken oval tub, testing the water, when Carol sneaked up on him, lifted his skirt and grabbed his todger.

Suzie, still hormonally difficult had protested. Perhaps a touch of the green eyed monster. She so immense, Carol so curvaceous.

"Don't keep playin' wiv me bloke like that," she had unreasonably scolded.

Carol bit. "Yer fuckin' invited me," she barked.

"I didn't invite yer just then," Suzie persisted unfairly.

Carol sprang up, facing Suzie. "No good yer keep changin' the goal posts gel. Either yer wants me to, or yer don't wants me to!"

"Movin'! Movin' the goal posts, yer dopey cow."

"Gawd! If yer weren't pregnant I'd slap yer face!"

"Looks as if yer need coolin' down Cas." Suzie placed a hand on Carol's shoulder. Then without warning shoved her. The blond went back, her foot slipping on the bath side. She toppled in, slapping the water arms outstretched. Everything was deluged within a six foot radius, soaking Jeff and depositing several gallons down the front of a startled Suzie.

Carol came up gasping for air. "Yer bitch!" she screamed.

Suzie clasped a hand to her face, then clutching her belly began to lose control, the giggles overcoming her.

That was too much. Carol had her friend by the ankle and pulled. Hopping frantically Suzie plunged in beside her. The pregnant girl sat in the water, hair plastered to her face. Jeff crouched laughing.

"What's so funny git?" Suzie snarled grabbing at the lad's hair. With her fist full she toppled him in.

Irritated by Carol's incessant cackle, Suzie scooped up a handful of suds and slapped them into her face. The blond blinked, cleared the foam from her eyes, glared at Suzie, then surrendered once more to the irresistible.

Suzie broke. The temper calmed, she joined her mate in hysteria. "I'm s…sorry g…gel," she stuttered. "Its me 'ormones. I…ignore me."

Regaining a modicum of control, Carol crossed her arms in front of her and seized the sodden tee-shirt's hem. She peeled it upward, over the unfortified bosom, their release captivating, and discarded the rag. Her skirt and panties followed suit.

Suzie submerged, a submariner's descent. Moments later Carol shuddered and let loose a gasp, a blissful leer replacing the initial look of shock. Suzie reappeared winking conspiratorially, her aspect smug.

All stripped to their birthday suits; Suzanne was the first to receive Jeff's undivided attention. Delicately he soaped her, deliberating on her swollen breasts, caressing, fingering the hard teats, before the rinse and oral attention.

Then after treating her back he asked her to stand. Soaping the ample bum he palmed the pleasing dunes, his finger seductively traversing the length of the separating fissure. From there he probed her Cheddar Gorge and delved the Wookey Hole, Suzie reciprocating with moans of unbound delight. The gentle hands slid down the inner thighs, she shivering with the touch.

Reclined once more Suzie offered a foot. Jeff received it promptly massaging the sole while he suckled the toes, one at a time, his lady teetering between giggles and sighs.

Carol, rather than merely observe, joined in, washing the bits of Jeff she could reach. She cuddled to his back, foam draped orbs cushioned to his wet skin. Her hands roamed that muscled torso, alighting upon a nipple, there she loitered, fingers teasing, stroking, finally to dip beneath the surface and fall upon the lurking Conger. Her grip firm about that excited denizen she rose, the horny poker unresisting.

That embrace intact, silky pubic locks then agitating sensitive buttocks, her hold on his salute to stimulation eased. The clenched hand moved forward, re-tightening about the crown. She squeezed, the sex probe throbbing with the clinch. Almost releasing him Carol slowly felt the whole shaft, until her hand touched the curls. Then she dipped to the seed sack; the warm gland nestled in her palm. She closed the gap, a digit feeling the compressed balls.

Leaving the rampant phallus, Carol sensuously stroked those buttocks, deliberating on how red they would soon prove to be, relishing the provocation of that scarlet blush, knowing she would be indulging his need. How different that was to sadistically whipping an unwilling victim, her mind momentarily dwelling on Cork and the Pegasus.

Carol recalled the cut of the cat of nine tails. How those knotted ligatures punished her naked body. How they burned like the fires of hell upon her unprotected flesh.

She remembered for how long those whip marks marred her body and the touch of clothing on those bloodied welts. She was glad she had shot him. Perhaps she should have given him a one way ticket to visit the devil.

That with Jeff was not vindictive. That was sexual play. That was a volcanic lust. His yearning she understood. Her experience with Gradowski the farmer had shown her pain could be transcended if the circumstances were right.

Cork had only ever instilled terror. She could never have felt anything other than sheer misery with him.

Carol dropped to her knees and moved to the lad's front, taking his stick of rock she eased the foreskin back and licked his end. Her tongue darted back and forth, agitating; waves of ecstasy consumed him, she was being careful not to bring him off.

Jeff repaid the courtesy with interest, studiously attending to every nook and cranny, lingering, wilfully in one particular cranny.

"Jeff." Suzie called for his attention as he finished with Carol.

He answered obediently. "Yes milady."

"Yer can drop that now." She smiled, glancing guiltily at Carol. "We'll only do that when we play, all right?"

Jeff's face lit up. "Yeah. Sure Sooze. Great!"

Carol winked at the reformed girlfriend.

"Now you ugly bastard, go get that new paddle we bought last week," Suzie growled. "We's gonna whip arse."

Jeff having vacated the bathroom, Carol reassured. "That's a first step babe."

"Yeah," Suzie agreed. "He's all right really. I'm just used to a bloke lordin' it that's all."

"Like Wayne? Or worse Cork?"

"Yeah, get what yer mean."

"Jeff's kind and considerate, now yer've straightened 'im out. Get used to it. Enjoy, he's nice."

The door flew open and the puffing Adonis rushed in, paddle in hand. He offered it to his mistress.

Taking it from him she said. "Yer bum's dry lover boy. I wants it nice and wet. Yer's gonna feel this so get yerself back in 'ere."

With Jeff re-immersed she continued. "That's it, nice an soppin'. Now Jeff, bend over the edge of the bath." She held the paddle under water while she fumbled in the pockets of her maternity smock. Finally she tugged an egg timer free. She placed it by Jeff, where he could watch its run.

She passed the paddle to Carol telling her. "Whack 'im good. Don't matter if he squeals. Thrash 'im until the sand runs out."

The implement consisted of a short wooden handle bound about a leather tongue. The business end measured some eight by three inches and appeared terribly thick.

Carol placed a hand on Jeff's lower back and raised the 'thrasher'. Suzie slipped between the lad's thighs and depressing his tool wrapped her mouth about his circumference.

The room echoed to the sound of tanned hide on soft flesh, a tremendous slap on proffered buttock, Carol choosing to beat the cheeks alternately. Jeff grimaced as the broadside from a swarm of bees tore through that decimated loin. His piece lurched in appreciation of the arousing fire and suckled cock.

Carol waited for his hurt to ebb before the second delivery, his flesh already blooming where the first had trespassed.

Whack! Jeff's rear shuddered to a third, the leather ripping into him above the scarlet of the first. His butt began to glow.

Whack! So far Carol had struck on virgin territory. Jeff yet had to feel the hard leather on scorched meat.

Suzie relented on her manipulations and surfacing for air proceeded to splash water onto Jeff's burning backside. "Keep 'im wet," she said. "It stings worse when yer wet." Jeff would have vouched for that, if another belter on the tops of his thighs had not deprived him of breath.

The paddle landed again, connecting abruptly with the scalded cheek, igniting further fires on the kindled rump. Hot needles pierced deep, kindling an inner sun that would soon cause another inferno to rage.

For three minutes, with ten second pauses that implement flashed down, the explosive slaps echoing perpetually about the tiled confines. Those scarlet mounds quivered with every delivery, the insatiable Jeff lusting, yearning, relishing each generous bum blasting discharge.

The sands ran out. "D'yer think he's 'ard boiled yet?" Carol asked of Suzie.

"He's 'ard I can vouch for that," the girl replied cheerfully. "An' 'is bum looks boiled. Like a lobster ain't it?" she commented laughing.

"I bet it stings like fuck, eh Jeff," Carol asked.

"It is a bit sore, yeah."

"Sore! Sore! Jeff darling you don't know the meaning of the word. Not yet anyway," Suzie cajoled. "Now you gets a real lickin' boy, an' I don't mean yer cock neither."

Suzie held the paddle high nodding to Carol to restart the egg timer. With powerful arm she hurtled the leather rectangle at those steaming cheeks, Jeff's backside shaking vigorously with the dynamic impact. He gasped as the new wave of brimstone coated that tormented behind, he was slowly being taken to the limit.

Suzie was a lot stronger than Carol and far more indiscriminate, Jeff feeling her deliberations more profoundly, his backside fast approaching boiling point. She did not wait for the pain to subside. Well versed by then in disciplinary techniques she pounded his backside. The paddle rising and falling in rapid succession. A steady swack! swack! swack! filling the room.

Carol watched mesmerised as the lad's buttocks danced their way to boiling point, his flesh cavorting to the macabre visitations. His fists clenched, white knuckled as Suzie punished his smarting hide.

But Jeff had not found purgatory; no he revelled in a sublime ecstasy. The continuous smart seemed to penetrate his groin, aggravating that organ, electrifying. His stiff ached with its rigidity, a hard ready to explode.

Every four seconds or so that implement scorched his backside. Fifteen hearty slaps to the minute. Forty-five flesh searing kisses to the session. Suzie whipped him until the last grain of sand fell to the pile below.

"Gawd!" Carol gasped, her hand firmly pressed to her ginger bush. "His bott don't 'alf look sore."

"Jealous?" Suzie asked suggestively.

"'Ow d'yer mean?" Carol demanded, taken aback.

"Thought you might like your fat arse whacked, that's all," she answered, her expression sly and inquisitive.

"You offering?" Carol prevaricated, giving her time to think.

"Can't you just feel your plump cheeks dancing to this?" As a demonstration Suzie welted Jeff's arse again. The lad tensed and moaned, he was still not back from paradise.

"To the egg timer?" Carol pointed to the glass.

"Yeah, to the egg timer," Suzie confirmed.

"Wet?" Carol massaged the smooth skin of her buttocks in anticipation.

"Wet," Suzie concurred.

Carol's groin tightened with the possibility. Suzie paddling her bare bum and before an excited Jeff appealed. To be held in subservience by her intimate and some times lover, her bottom fervently warmed thrilled. But she felt it could be even better.

"Later," she decided, an impish smile indicating connivance.

"If that's what yer wants gel."

"Yer can do it proper. Runaway slave in chains gets tied to the post an' whipped for her troubles."

"Whipped!" Suzie exclaimed.

"Yeah. Clothes torn from me quiverin' body."

"An' chained to the whippin' post," Suzie added.

"So me 'eels is off the ground," Carol continued, the excitement rising.

56

"An' taught a lesson yer won't forgets."

"Me bare arse lashed by the master."

"While 'is snooty wife watches."

"Then given a shaftin' for good measure."

"While the bitch of a wife continues to punish yer welted arse wiv a horsewhip."

"Yeah......Sooze?"

"What Cas?"

"Me cunt's gone all of a quiver."

"Don't worry gel, Jeff'll shoot 'is arrow into it soon," Suzie promised grinning. "Now shall we finish what we started. Phase three of." She welted the lad's bum again. "'Is bum blisterin' spankin'. You sit yerself on a chair and get face ache over yer lap. Yer can whack 'im wiv the leather and I, I've got a special for 'im."

Having organised part three of her boyfriend's punishment roster, she awkwardly removed herself from the bath and padded from the room.

Carol's big blue eyes connected with Jeff's. She smiled provocatively. "Yer've 'ad the slap matey," she mewed. "'Ow d'yer fancy some tickle?"

Jeff's response came without hesitation. "With you, any time."

Spontaneously they embraced. Bodies entwined. Lips met tentatively, then with a burning desire. Hands cupped her buttocks pulling her tight to him her breasts flattening to his chest. Tongues investigated, tasting, relishing each other. His stiff ached between her thighs, longing to travel the tunnel of love; the shaft nestled to her sex. Carol rocked back and forth enjoying that rigid member, furthering the desire.

"God! I don't half want you Cas," Jeff confided, his intent quite obvious.

"Patience," she urged, assuring him he would.

Suzie returned surprising them, they having been lost in time and their embrace.

"You at it again?" she remarked, striving to be inoffensive that time. She held a short birch bundle in her clenched fist.

Parting, slightly embarrassed, though for no real reason, the couple climbed from the tub and took up their agreed positions, Jeff laying almost eagerly across the proffered thighs.

The timer set, Carol lambasted the fired butt, that quickly followed by a swipe from Suzie's birch. Jeff hardened further with the intensity of the assault, his backside a frenzy, a hotbed of stinging red hot needles.

Slap! Whack! Slap! Whack! Slap! Whack! So Jeff received, writhing not in agony but with the imminence of his forthcoming orgasm

Slap! Carol tended those inflamed buttocks

Whack! Suzie switched to his unblemished thighs. That new assault very nearly finished him. How his legs smarted, the twigs raking the tender flesh.

Slap! Whack! Slap! Whack! That punishment continued relentless. The buzz in his groin expanded. Then as the allotted time neared the end his ball tightened, triggering a spasmodic flow of milky juices, his cock delivering the seed to Carol's thighs. Hot and sticky it trickled slowly down her leg.

Carol placed a cool hand on the heated derriere. "Enjoyed it did yer?" she asked. "I've a good mind to make yer lick the stuff off." Jeff rose in relaxed frame of mind his cock still secreting his come.

Figure Chapter 6 Looking For Carol

6-Looking For Carol

Cork located Carol's address with extreme ease, her name clearly listed in the telephone directory for Greater London under C.A.Widney. He noted the road and flat number.

"Well miss high and fucking mighty gun toting trollop, have I got a treat for you!" That promise he whispered closing the post office door. He stared down at the damaged arm hung by his side. Slowly he lifted it until the hand was before his face. He studied that a moment, then flexed the fingers. He formed a fist, swung about and smashed that knuckle sandwich through a fence panel. Withdrawing he reiterated. "Oh yes have I got a treat for you."

Ten minutes later Cork had purchased an A to Z from a newsagents. He thumbed through it finding the road in Fulham. Within half an hour he had parked the stolen Jaguar in a position to observe the three story building, heedless of the double yellow line he had stopped on.

An hour drifted by. The postman came and went. A traffic warden strolled toward him booking the odd illegally parked vehicle. Cork drove around the block several times until the official had gone. The last thing he wanted was a confrontation. That time he was more fortunate, an old Peugeot estate vacated a space by a meter as Cork neared.

That meter loaded, Cork ascended the steps to the front door of number ninety two, Clapham road. The house had been converted to flats, six in all. Lettered A to F.

'Must be a pokey hole,' Cork mused. *'Still what more can a tart want?'* Laughing at his own joke he pressed the bell to Carol's flat.

A male voice answered. "Yeah."

"Parcel for C. Widney," Cork lied.

"Okay mate. Come up," the voice instructed.

'Too easy,' thought Cork. *'She isn't there.'*

He climbed the bare wood stairs to the second floor and knocked on flat E.

"It's open," the male called out. Cork walked in.

A fresh faced youth, eyes blacked and a sticking plaster over the bridge of his nose, squatted on the floor sorting through a pile of compact discs. He glanced up asking. "Where's the parcel then?"

"A fib," Cork admitted. "I'm looking for Carol."

"Don't tell me you're her new fancy man. Well she ain't here mate. Gone to that barmpot friend of hers I expect," the Young man guessed.

"Ah, Suzanne! Yes?"

"Yeah. They're welcome to each other if you ask me. They're both round the bend."

"Where can I find Suzanne these days?" Cork ventured.

"Fuck knows. She's packed her flat up and gone off somewhere."

"No idea where I suppose?"

"You're askin' a lot of questions ain't yer mate?"

"I need to find Carol. It is a matter of some urgency," Cork imparted adamant.

"And I said I don't know." The Young man continued with his sorting.

"Who are you? Her ex?"

"None of your business."

"You aren't stealing those records are you?" The policeman in him had to ask.

"They're mine. I just haven't got around to sorting them out," the lad defended.

Either the Young man had no idea of Carol's whereabouts or was not saying. Cork tried a different tack. "Has Carol an address book?"

"If she has you ain't seein' it."

"I see. Stand up for a minute will you," Cork requested smiling.

The lad climbed to his feet faced Cork and rasped. "What?"

Cork laid him flat with one punch to the jaw. Before he could regain his wits to retaliate Cork placed the soul of his boot between the man's legs and applied a little pressure.

"Now let us begin again. We seem to have a slight misunderstanding between us. Or you have an attitude problem. My name is John Cork. You may or may not have heard of me. It is of no consequence either way.

I want that flighty trollop Widney and I *will* find her sooner or later, one way or another. If you assist my enquiries I won't crush your bollocks. Now are we on the same wavelength?"

Nursing a bruised jaw the fellow stared up at the ogre towering above him. That arm hanging by his side. The curly receding hairline. The insane expression. And oh! The revolver butt protruding from his waistband. The lad nodded.

"You are Wayne aren't you?" Cork asked. Wayne nodded again. "I thought so. You look the pathetic type. Now Wayne, where is she?"

"Cornwall," Wayne blurted without hesitation.

"Good. An address?"

"I honestly don't know."

Cork lowered his boot heel. Wayne gurgled, his face contorted. "I see. I believe you Wayne. Even you couldn't be as stupid as to lie to me. Especially when your balls are within an inch of ceasing to exist. An address book if you please."

"Aaaahghh. Top right h...hand d...d...drawer behind you."

"Thank you lad." Cork turned and opened the drawer saying as he did. "Stay Wayne. I don't want to have to hurt you again."

Cork plucked the book from the drawer and thumbed through it. "Ah!" He exclaimed at length. "Suzanne Dixon. Oh and a pleasant part of the country too. Only a few miles from my last home too."

Placing the booklet in his pocket he withdrew the revolver and pointed it at Wayne. "So sorry, lad," he whispered. "But I can't afford the Old Bill knowing where I'm bound."

Wayne didn't even get the chance to scream. He died immediately.

"Easy Peasy," Cork muttered. "Killing scum is no problem at all."

Nobody heard the shot. There was not a soul at home. Cork fired the Jaguar's engine and headed West out of town.

"Am I permitted to speak?" Jeff asked of Suzie.

"Course you are love," she answered, her hand ruffling his hair. "Anytime yer wants."

"This is just an idea mind you." His expression was childlike, he was eager to please: "What if we go into Plymouth. Stay for a few days. Go clubbing, have a good time. We could stay with Gus. I'm sure he wouldn't mind." The words were babbled as if his new found freedom was to be short lived.

Suzie immediately seized on the idea. "Yeah Jeff. I'd like that."

"Are yer sure?" Carol questioned the decision. "I mean in your state an' all. What if Zac decides to come into the world in the midst of double vodkas and the dance of the whales? And who's Gus?"

"Look nurse Widney. First off I don't drink anymore. Second off watch who you're callin' a whale. Third off who invited you anyway? And last off Gus is an old mate of Jeff's."

In quick response to Carol's lip trembler Jeff added. "Of course you're invited Cas. Don't be so rotten Sooze…….."

"She started it, callin' me a whale," Suzie defended.

Jeff ignored her interruption. "Gus is an old university friend. In fact he was my only uni friend. In fact," he continued, looking downcast. "He's my *only* mate, end of story."

"Nah he ain't," Carol chirruped. "You got Sooze an' me ain't yer?"

"Yeah," he agreed the despondency lifting. "And won't Gus be green when he meets you!"

"Will he?" Carol asked surprised. "Why? Is he ill or something?"

"Envious Cas. Envious."

"Just takin' the piss," she said with a grin.

"'Ere," Suzie piped up. "What about me? I knows I'm the size of a whale." She glared momentarily at Carol. "But ain't I got nuffin' to be green about?"

"Course yer 'ave gel," Carol answered tongue in cheek. "A belly the size of Wembley Arena an' an arse to fit a wide bodied Jumbo jet."

"You can talk wiv them cow's udders 'angin' on yer chest miss fuckin' perfect. You just wait until yer chained to that whippin' post. I'll see to it the master decorates that dainty little backside of yours wiv a nice pattern of red stripes."

"Eh?"

"Yer forgot ain't yer?"

"Oh Christ!"

"He won't 'elp yer either. Don't want spankin' yer says. I wants whippin'. Run away slave in chains gets tied to the post an' whipped for her troubles yer says. Clothes torn from me quiverin' body yer says. Me bare arse lashed by the master. Shall I go on?"

"No. Okay we'll do it. Nothin' too 'eavy though."

"Course not," Suzie concurred, deceit written all over her face. "Now?"

"Yeah all right." Carol wasn't sure at all.

As the threesome retired to dress for their game Cork stopped at a petrol station on the A30 two miles East of Honiton.

A leggy redhead dressed in leather jacket and jeans leant casually against the wall of the service station shop.

Holding the collar of her jacket to her neck, shivering she smiled at Cork.

The escaped convict, sadist and by then cold blooded murderer, paid his bill, purchased a snack and two hot coffees. Leaving the building he offered one of those steaming beverages to the Young woman.

"Well it's not sweets I suppose," she said taking it from him.

"You need a lift?" Cork inquired.

"Yeah as it happens."

"Going far?"

"How far do you want to go?" she asked, her question full of innuendo.

"As far as you will allow," he answered his face dead pan.

"I had a row with my boyfriend," she explained feeling her situation needed that. "The bastard dumped me two miles down the bloody road. Me feet are killing me."

"Life's full of disappointments," he remarked offering a sandwich. "Motorcyclist?"

"Yeah," she replied accepting the offer. "Took me helmet and all."

"So you're looking for a shag?" Cork asked bluntly.

"Yer don't mess about do you mister?"

"Is that all you wanted, or was there something else?"

"I need a lift into Oakhampton. I'm willing to be good company if you happen to be going my way."

"I believe we can come to some arrangement," Cork affirmed striding away to his car, the girl hurriedly following discarding the polystyrene cup as she did so.

Driving from the forecourt Cork asked. "What game do you play?"

"Straight in and out. I've got a pack in me pocket."

"What if I wanted to tie you to a tree, flog your arse with a birch and then bugger you?" He smiled.

"You got a weird sense of humour mate."

"Don't fancy that then?"

"You're not serious!" She searched his face frowning, checking his intent. Cork as usual was unreadable.

Twenty minutes down the road the teenager sniffed, then sniffed again. She sneezed and reached for the glove compartment. "You got a tissue in here?" she asked. Before Cork could prevent her she had pulled down the cover. "Bloody hell! What's this? She removed the gun.

"A toy," Cork replied unflustered. "Realistic isn't it? It's my son's."

"Oh right." She aimed it at Cork's head and shouted. "Bang! Bang!" Luckily for Cork and for her she didn't pull the trigger, although she did no favours for his heart beat and bowel.

Cork held his hand out, receiving the gun in his open palm. Something about the man said 'don't fuck with me'. Deciding then was the right moment Cork turned off the main road and drove the quiet lanes searching for a suitable location. Slowing he turned the car onto a rutted cart track, following that into a grove of trees. Birch trees.

"What's your name girl?" Cork asked, switching off the engine.

"Lisa."

Cork rubbed his chin. "Well Lisa. I lied to you. A habit I'm getting into lately. You see if you had pulled the trigger of this little toy, you would have spread my brains all over the car."

"It's real?"

"Oh yes. If you could ask young Wayne you would know just how devastating it is. But sadly for Wayne you can't. You see Lisa I killed him this morning."

She laughed. "No," she said, rejecting his admission. "You're really weird you are. If you don't mind I'll walk from here. Thanks for the lift. You see I lied too. You were never getting inside my knickers. You never stood a cat in hell's chance."

"Oh Lisa, dear sweet harlot, I do mind. I wasn't joking about birching you."

"You're sick. Off your trolley. 'Round the fucking bend," she gasped with fear.

Cork's reactions were quick. His hand went to her throat pushing her into her seat, the revolver barrel pressed in to the cheek of an ashen face. "Unfortunately the only way I can demonstrate the truth of the matter is by shooting you. I really don't want to waste the bullet. I only have five you see. I shall require at least another two.

Now I shall provide you with a sharp knife. Like a good girl you will go out and cut a dozen straight ends about two and a half feet in length, from those young trees over there." He indicated with his finger. "I shall be watching. One false move and....." He leaned forward and yelled in her face. "**Bang! Bang!**" Releasing his grip he gave her a penknife he had found in the car.

Terrified, shaking uncontrollably, Lisa set about her task. Darkness was only an hour away and the temperature was dropping. The twigs collected she returned to Cork.

"What now?" she asked, teeth chattering.

Cork passed her a piece of string. "Tie that about the base. Bind them to form a handle. Top to bottom and not too tight. The ends should spread so as to cover more of your bottom. The penknife please."

The bunch so bound, she stared not daring to ask what next. Cork busied himself trimming the twigs. Finally content he said. "Take off your clothes please."

"You're kiddin'. It's bloody freezin'"

"Do you want me to shoot you?"

Lisa threw off her jacket, pausing to glare at Cork.

"All of your clothes Lisa. Keep pissing me about and I'll give you extras."

Thoughtfully she unfastened the button of her jeans, the zipper slid slowly down. She peeled the denim from her hips and thighs, kicking off the leather boots she wore; she stepped from the jeans.

Cork scrutinised the long shapely legs as he lit a cigarette. As an afterthought he offered one to Lisa. Puzzled she took it.

"Can I keep the rest of me togs on please mister? Please."

"Lisa you are annoying me. Six extra. Does that answer your question?"

Heartless he watched her drag the thick woollen jumper over her head, reducing her to red lacy bra, panties and knee length socks.

She unfastened the brassiere, tossing it to the ground with the rest of her clothes. Her shapely breasts trembled with that movement and her constant shivering. With a look of dread and resignation she dropped her panties.

Cork had followed her strip with a keen interest. "You can keep your socks on," he ventured grinning. "Nice pair of tits Lisa. Is your bum as firm? Turn around and let me see." Lisa obeyed. "Ah, just as I had hoped. Exquisite." His rough hand caressed the roundness. "I shall enjoy flogging you."

"I'm cold mister. Let me go please," she begged, hugging herself.

"I don't think I could stand the disappointment." He unzipped his fly and eased his stiff into the open. "See what you have done to me. Kiss it Lisa."

The girl's bottom lip trembled. Grudgingly she knelt, leant forward and lightly pecked the head.

"Pull the foreskin back."

Lisa did so.

"Lick my prick girl."

Her tongue touched the glistening dome.

66

"Lick it properly." Cork's hand reached to her buttocks. As she pleasured him he helped himself, groping the smooth skin of her stretched behind.

"Suck me Lisa," he whispered. Her soft lips slid over his circumference. His hand wandered to her breasts, squeezing and mauling. "That's it girl. Good strong sucks. Give me heaven."

Lisa had other ideas however. Frightened for her hide, terrified for her life, she sank her teeth into his piece. Then to add injury to injury she punched him hard in the balls as she reared from the stricken phallus.

"Bitch!" Cork roared, nursing the violent hurt. "You're dead. Do you hear me? Dead!"

Immobilised with pain he watched helpless as she rapidly gathered her clothes and ran into the surrounding trees, her plump white backside disappearing into the undergrowth.

Recovering he surveyed the surrounding landscape, then starting the car said to himself. "I wonder if the bitch has any brains?"

He backed the Jag back out of the grove and onto the lane. Then he drove for a half mile in the direction Lisa had taken. The late afternoon became gloomier by the minute. He had to find the run away quickly before the terrain became to dark to see in.

Lisa had run her heart out. The barren winter undergrowth had taken its toll of her sock covered feet. She ran for eight hundred yards before collapsing in a breathless heap. Sports had never been her strong point. In fact she did not excel in any particular sphere.

The soles of her feet pained her. Inspection proved she had been cut up quite badly on her dash for freedom. Desperately she dressed; the clothes adhering to her sweat soaked body. Fear gripped her gut. Where was he? Where was the bastard? Lisa could hear no sound of him. A muted wintry silence surrounded her.

Nearly a thousand yards from her squatted Cork. Puffing on a cigarette he watched, as if without a care in the world. Cork looked and listened for the telltale sign that would give away Lisa's presence.

Lisa did not have the wits to circle back. She was terrified, a frightened animal and frightened animals run directly away from their predators. She peered into the gloom then continued to follow the same path.

Twigs cracked beneath her boots, firecrackers in the absolute silence. All the time her way became less easy to see. She was not within earshot of Cork as she stumbled dramatically on.

Cork's first indication of Lisa's whereabouts came when a rabbit bolted from bushes some hundred and fifty yards to his left. His hand tightened on the grip of the revolver. His cigarette he immediately extinguished.

Ten minutes he reckoned before the light faded completely. Ten minutes to apprehend the devious bitch. Birds flew from a tree two hundred yards to his fore.

"Gotcha!" Cork moved fast and silent over the light undergrowth, aiming for a point one hundred and fifty yards to the right of where the bird had taken flight.

Lisa, her chest aching, struggled on. Tears wetted her face, those mixing with the sweat of her exertions.

Her feet blazed, the damage done before replacing her boots. The socks red with blood, the soles of her feet cut by the woodland debris. Branch ends played callously with her face, etching their own marks to that flushed mascara stained countenance.

A small clearing opened before her. The dismal light improved slightly. She paused, breath condensing in the cold evening air. Doubling, clutching her gut to counter the stitch, her staccato breath rasping in her throat, she turned and peered back into those eerie depths.

"**Bang! Bang!**" shouted from nearby froze her. Terror seized, incapacitating. Without moving she knew. Unable even to scream she whispered. "No! Please God no!"

"Want to meet him in person?" Cork's cold voice asked.

"Please mister. Don't kill me. I'll do anything. Honest I will."

"Anything eh? Put your hands behind your back and don't try anything this time." Cork secured her with his tie.

"Now turn around," he ordered quietly.

As she faced Cork, he slapped her face with the flat of his hand, knocking her head to one side. As a trickle of blood coursed down her chin Cork said. "That's for the bite. Believe me girl you are going to kiss it better. And you'll pay dearly for that right hook. I am going to flay you alive. Dwell on that." He grabbed her by the jacket and dragged her back to the car.

"You can sit in the front, but any tricks and you'll go in the boot, get me?"

Lisa nodded, thankful the retribution was billed for later.

68

Figure Chapter 7 If You Asks You Gets

7-If You Asks You Gets

The master attired in long black frock coat, lacy shirt and gold waistcoat busied himself at his desk, reading and signing important papers purporting to the vast Tennessee cotton farm he owned.

The door to his study opened. A chained female stumbled into the room, pushed by a whip wielding tyrant in jodhpurs and white blouse.

"The runaway sir," she announced.

"So I see Dixon. You burst in here again without knocking and **you** will feel that whip on your hide," the man scolded.

He arrogantly perused the young woman before him. "Well Widney what am I to do with you? Tell me, why did you run? Don't you care for life at Bridge Plantation? Do we not treat you well?"

The young woman answered not. She concentrated on her feet. She was bound by heavy iron manacles, her ankles hobbled and connected by strong links. A similar arrangement held her wrists, the two sets connected by more chain. She humbled herself before her owner, shoeless and wearing only a flimsy skirt and blouse.

Mistress Dixon, the foreman lay her crop to the girl's butt. "Answer," she barked.

Wincing from the sharp connection she spoke. "Don't like being beaten," she offered as reason.

"I see. I shall remember that when I mete out your punishment girl." He looked at Dixon. "Where did you find this untrustworthy peasant?"

"Down by Coppice swamp master. Frightened to go in and scared of coming back sir."

"Perhaps when you feel the lash on your naked back you'll wish you had chanced the 'gators."

"Are you going to whip me then sir?" the girl asked warily.

"What do you think? You haven't been here five minutes. I paid a handsome figure for your handsome figure. Two hundred dollars. I expect you to work damned hard, not to go gallivanting as soon as the opportunity arises, because you are work shy."

Master Bridges rose, a daunting figure, and walked with deliberation around the desk, continuing his tirade. "I have three hundred slaves on this plantation. I cannot afford them the privilege of believing they can run off and simply get away with it. No, you shall be made an example of. I shall deal with you in the severest manner."

70

"How many lashes sir?" she asked meekly.

"As many as I care to give you. I guarantee you won't lie on your back for some days though."

"Please sir don't whip me. I won't run no more. I promise. I'll work ever so hard. You see if I don't," she begged and pleaded.

"Too late for regret. You should have considered the consequence before you went walk about. Dixon, take her to the whipping post. Chain her to it. I shall be along shortly."

"Shall I strip her first sir?" Dixon inquired.

"No," Bridges replied, a smile twisting his lips. "I shall do that."

"Can I ask where we're going?" Lisa ventured.

"You can ask," Cork replied curtly.

"Where we going then?" Diplomacy was not Lisa's strong point.

"I don't suppose it matters. Cornwall, to visit an old acquaintance."

"You need a gun for that?"

"Yes I need a gun. You see I have an old score to settle."

"What happened to your arm?"

"That's the old score."

"What happened?" Lisa persisted.

"A whore shot me. But she's going to pay the price. I've already killed her boyfriend."

"Why?"

"Because he was there. Wrong time, wrong place."

"Ain't yer worried the police will catch you?"

"You **can** rabbit can't you?"

"Sorry. I'm nervous. I always talk a lot when I'm nervy. What are you going to do to me?"

"I haven't decided yet. But whatever it is it will hurt."

"You're a mean son of a bitch. Did ever anyone tell you that?"

"Frequently."

"Are you going to kill me?"

"Haven't decided."

"I know too much don't I?"

"Yes."

Lisa fell into a thoughtful silence.

Widney hung in chains, her heels clear of the hard wooden floor. Her manacles fastened to a ring bolted to the thick post above her head.

"I'm gonna enjoy watchin' the master cut you to pieces," Dixon promised. "That old whip he uses hurts like fuck!"

"Does yer think they said fuck a hundred years ago Sooze?"

"Don't know, don't care. An' don't call me Sooze, Cas. You'll spoil the act. Jeff likes it to seem real."

"Sorry Sooze."

"Yeah Cas."

They fell silent as the boots of the master sounded in the hallway outside. He strode purposefully in. "Time to taste the bite of leather," he announced.

Bridges took a knife from a pocket and sliced the material of her shirt bottom to top. He cut the fold of the collar, then piece by piece tore the shirt from her body. She clung to her chains naked to the waist.

Unable to resist the temptation he slipped his hands about her ribs and cupped the large breasts, feeling their firmness.

"Humility and pain are your punishments. You must learn you are no more than a mere chattel, to use as I see fit," he said.

His hands traversed her stomach, locating the button of the skirts waistband. That he undid. The garment fell to the floor. Her naked buttocks protruded tantalisingly for him.

His finger delved the cleft, feeling the warm skin, the yielding texture of her flesh. "I'm going to have you later Widney," he promised.

Dixon passed the master his whip, the leather polished, ungiving and hard, the tip fifty centimetres of pure hell. That four millimetres in diameter. The plaited leather then gradually thickened toward the grip, discoloured by use and twenty five millimetres thick.

Widney shivered. Not from cold or fear. No, that was from the sensation that thrilled her groin. Bound in chains, the clothes torn from her body; naked and at the mercy of another, her charms on display. All were contributing factors if you are made that way.

A severe and lengthy whipping promised, the leather raping her flesh. A protracted smart the calling card leaving her very substance fired from without and within.

Bridges composed himself, studying the sun kissed hide. A dull mauve line evidence of Dixon's curt swipe, split in two halves by the dip of her buttock cleft, decorated the plump dunes.

Bridges raised that scourge, flicking the tail behind him. Dixon watched intent, excitedly waiting on the first impact. She had grown to appreciate particular sadistic fancies. There was definitely something about the solid thwump of implement on human anatomy. Especially the well coated parts and all the better if that flesh were young and firm.

Bridges powered the beast forward, the tip slicing air, the ether whistling with its passing. The demon hit with a muted splat, curling to her shape, leaving a line of fire to her far hip.

"Shit!" Widney cursed, as the full import struck home, shaking the flesh, igniting the first flames of scalding ire.

The second, no improvement, fell low catching the very base of her bum cheeks, the tip taking its toll of her upper thighs.

"Fuck!" she hissed.

"Did they say that a hundred years ago?" Dixon unusually quick, asked sarcastically.

Bridges glared as Widney giggled through her suffering. "Do you want to stand alongside Dixon?" he asked suitably stern. Dixon shook her head indicating the negative. "Then be quiet!" he barked.

The next bedevilled, the stroke harder it seemed. Widney's rump quivered to the punishing lash; two colourful stripes grew deeper in colour, that third first creating a white line before it too turned red.

Bridges launched another rump shuddering incursion. That sting approached the intolerable. Widney's hips thrust forward, her groin ground against the post, her back arched, her body rigid and as the violence waned the master dealt another. Widney squirmed, the whip's mark torturing, lingering. She writhing tight against that post, the resulting sensations not unpleasant.

She groaned as number six raised an eight inch welt, the lower portion of her rump having played host to all the incursions thus far.

"Oh master, pray have mercy," Widney managed between gritted teeth.

"Mercy? Indolence is not served by mercy wench, but by the lash to quicken your step. How dare you ask me for mercy! Not only does thou evade thy duty, but thy begs forgiveness to evade thy rightful punishment!

Nay, I shall not be merciful. I shall flog thee until I can find no further flesh free from the whip's harsh education. Now quiet I say and receive with gratitude your correction."

With those words still hanging in the tense atmosphere, Bridges lay a butt slicer to the top of those tortured mounds, a downward stroke that imparted a fearful slap and an ensuing agonising smart, the demon's tip wickedly whipping vertically down her right haunch.

Widney cried out as the fires raged, smothering her scorched hide, a hideous welt rising to the occasion. Her contorted features turned to face Bridges and she mouthed "Thank you."

An idea entered the sadistic catacombs of the master's devious mind. "Perhaps I am wrong after all," he said.

"Eh?" Dixon grunted open mouthed.

"Whipping the fair young wench in this manner. It is not right."

"Ain't it?" questioned the dumbfounded brunette.

"Nay. Not right at all. It is quite clear she does not appreciate this particular lesson. Therefore I shall show her another. She shall be laid over the horse. Nay spread eagled and she shall feel the full benefit of my leather friend across her hind quarters."

Widney was summarily taken down from the post by a gleeful Dixon and dragged to the odious wooden structure. There she was bound; her warm buttocks positioned for a downward cut of the master's vile messenger.

"Now wench," said Bridges. "Thy shall thank me for each mark of your enlightenment."

"Oh verily master," quipped Dixon, tongue in cheek. "Whilst thy flog her between those fine fleshy thighs?"

"Who's to say obedient servant where the fine plaited tail shall land. Though I do admit she is finely displayed there."

"I do my best oh handsome one."

Widney stared wide-eyed listening to the conversation, the floor inches from her nose. She lay supported by a leather covered padding, legs spread to their limit and tied to the rear supports of the trestle, her hands were similarly bound to the front. A thick belt over her lower back held her firm and bowed.

She absorbed the implications of their words. Whip her cunt? Is that what they meant? The prospect thrilled, but the pain? It would be unbearable in practise. Surely the master wouldn't, would he?

"Don't her boobs 'ang nice master?" Dixon was saying. "Wouldn't they dance nicely to the lash?"

"Perhaps we might find out Dixon," the master suggested. Unbeknown to Widney the pair were on a wind up, her backside the only intended target.

Widney was dragged from her lustful cogitations by the whistle of the lash's tail. The crack of leather on stretched flesh jarred her mental receptors, a branding infinitely worse than previously dealt.

"Thank you sir," she squealed.

The smart persevered as a second struck, the thong cutting both cheeks. There was no evading that scathing discipline, her body held rigid; the skin taut over the muscles of her behind, no plump fat to absorb the shock. She couldn't even thrust forward with the descending devil.

Again she yelped a strangled acknowledgment.

Bridges whipped her arse from top to bottom and bottom to top coating that sphere with a carpet of welts, that scarlet arse aflame with pain and desire.

If Widney believed her master finished, she was mistaken. He harboured ill intent toward her well striped derriere.

Bridges moved to her fore, raised the implement and dealt a flesh shuddering vertical stroke, the mean end raising a welt down her thigh.

Widney had transcended pain. Each whiplash added to the boil in her groin. She could have endured for ever. Her mind reeled. The combining factors raised her pulse and fired her organ. The spread position. The whipping. Her audience, if only it were unknown faces watching her humiliation.

With her vagina on display and that sensuous flagellator getting ever closer her mind screamed for it. She longed for, lusted for that supple plaited leather to cut about her scarlet arse and flay her cunt. To be whipped there, the centre of her desire. For that to sting, to smart, to reach beyond that wet chasm and smack her pubic mound, so her mind sank ever deeper into the abyss of depravation.

Bridges however was mindful not to lash her there, fearful of the damage he might incur.

Having flogged her from left to right he ceased. "You may release the prisoner now," he told Dixon.

Widney stood, her hands flying to her rear. She felt the mass of ridges; those meticulously raised so as not to break the skin.

"Are you contrite Widney?" Bridges asked.

"Am I sorry d'yer mean?"

"Exactly."

"No."

"What exactly do you mean by no?" he snarled.

"I'm not sorry I ran. I'd do it again given half the chance."

"Am I hearing right? Do you want another flogging?"

"I'll not lie."

"Very commendable I'm sure. What say you Dixon?"

"Flog the bitch some more," she replied.

"Do you want that Widney?"

The young woman smiled and nodded. "So close," she whispered.

"Then where do you suggest I lay it? Your back?"

Again Widney smiled; her hand stroked the tight ginger curls and then her breasts.

"I see. Perhaps I might accommodate you." He considered the possibility, a noticeable bulge appearing within the tight trousers. "On her knees Dixon, back to that cross over there."

The cross mentioned was attached to a short upright and leant at an angle. The legs of the 'X' clear of the ground to permit her calves to pass beneath. Widney was strapped to that, kneeling, leaning backwards. Her arms were secured outstretched above her head, the centre of the 'X' crossing at the small of her back, above the hot buttocks.

Bridges selected a shorter, lighter whip and approached the wistful captive. She closed her eyes in blissful anticipation as the master raised the scourge, her groin buzzing in excitement.

A slight whisper pursued the path of the speeding leather tail, which struck with devastating consequence upon the fragile substance of the inner thigh. Widney inhaled sharply, gasping as the burning smart consumed her erotic thoughts.

Not enough! How could she tell the master she required to be abused with more energy?

The whip revisited, closer to the centre of arousal that time. Widney glanced up at her antagonist and poked her tongue out. She certainly felt the impact of his next delivery, a veritable scorcher along the joint of thigh and pubic mound, following the curve of her sex to lick deliciously upon the underside of her ravaged bottom.

Widney gasped with the significance of that visitation. The sting penetrated, drove remorselessly into her organ, the electric buzz expanded.

Still not enough. Whatever Bridges dealt her would be insufficient. Images pierced her disturbed state. The leather licked her cunt; the ensuing smart engulfed her tender lips. She reeled, the lust in her obscene, yearning for draconian measures.

She visualised the red hot smouldering 'T' of a branding iron being pressed into her moist vagina. The sizzle of scorched flesh, the dreadful consequence taking her to Nirvana.

The whip lashed her soft labia. The exquisite sensation between her legs boiled, grew and then shrank. So close. So near and yet so far.

The mind's eye saw her bent over naked in public. Strapped. No, tied with rough rope to a hitching rail, her arms horizontal and secured so tight. Her legs were opened to their widest. A man, no a cowboy with heated iron singeing her bare behind. A suitable punishment for, yes the iron withdrew, *'WHORE'* branded on her cheek.

Eyes tight to the world, every muscle taut she felt the first incursion to her breast. More images flitted through her conscious.

Hells Angels ripping the clothes from her.

The breast stung madly, the orb danced wildly.

They held her flat on her back, her legs in the air. Greasy monsters mauled her breasts while a gargantuan Neolithic beast with a massive ram forced his entry, her arse hole screaming at the intrusion.

Still that fulfilment evaded her. Her chest decorated with a maze of livid stripes, she opened her eyes to see Bridges inert, whip hand by his side.

"I can't do any more Cas," he explained apologetically. "Look at your body. You're a mess."

"Oh Jeff, I got so near. I reckon if I had it would 'ave been mind blowin'. I would never have believed that being whipped could be so erotic. The thoughts I 'ad, they were disgustin'."

"Tell us," prompted Suzie.

"Nah, too embarrassin' Sooze. It would pollute that squidgy clean pea of yours."

"Watch it gel. You ain't untied yet."

"Yer could flog me 'til the cows come 'ome Sooze. I can't get enough."

"Yeah, we noticed. Jeff is right though yer can't take no more. It'll be days before them marks go."

"Yeah Sooze. Jeff fuck me. Shag me tied to this cross. Rape me. I gotta come now. I'm flyin' ten mile high."

Jeff did not require asking twice. His meat was quickly produced, stiff as the proverbial board. He had her there, the long awaited orgasm finally 'blowin' 'er mind'.

Figure 9 Chapter 8 Goings and Comings

8-Goings and Comings

Suitcases packed Carol cautiously perched on the edge of the dining room table. Suzanne smiled sympathetically.

"I'm surprised yer can sit at all. Yer bum was just a mass of welts at the finish. Sore are yer?"

"A bit. Can't wear no knicks. Me fanny's too sore. Can't wear no bra either. It's weird Sooze, when Jeff were whippin' me I couldn't get enough. He could 'ave lashed any bit he pleased and I would 'ave enjoyed it. But now I feel sort of......"

"Ashamed? Dirty? Sorry?" Suzie offered.

"Sort of, but not exactly. No I feel, I wish me body weren't marked. I feel, I feel like a slut."

"That's not surprising is it? You are a slut."

"Thanks mate. 'Ow did you feel at first?"

"Humiliated an' fuckin' mad. The git never asked did he? He just took liberties."

"No, I mean when yer let 'im do it."

"I've always been a tart Cas. A free thinkin' slut though. If I likes it, I does it. I don't 'ave no regrets."

"Yeah. I guess that's the way to see it," Carol agreed.

"Any way **what was** going through yer mind?"

"Gawd! Yer'll be shocked!"

"So shock me."

"First I imagined Jeff brandin' me love 'ole. Then a cowboy branded me bare arse wiv the word whore in front of the whole town. Then I was bein' raped and buggered by a gang of dirty, mean Hell's Angels. Disgustin' ain't I?"

"Worse. Yer sick more like it. Though I wouldn't mind the last bit meself. Where were these buggers?"

"Git!"

"Slut!"

"Brainless tart!"

"Baggage!"

"Brazen hussy!"

"Whore!"

"Arse hole!"

Jeff wandered into the room, listening to the exchange. "Best of mates as usual I see," he remarked casually.

"Course we is," Carol quickly countered. "It's only bestest mates that can call each uvver the things we do."

"Yeah," agreed Suzie. "When I call Cas a flighty trollop wiv a mouth like a sewer it's cos I love 'er."

"Yeah. An' when I call Sooze a thick scrubber with a cock permanently between 'er legs, it's cos I love 'er."

Jeff laughed. "I see. And what would you call one another if you hated each other?"

"The case don't come up," Carol retorted.

"Time we left girls. I have rung the housekeeper to say we are off for a few days. She will come around later and house sit while we are away."

"What about 'er family?" Carol inquired.

"She has none. A spinster is Jane. Forty two and never bedded."

"'Ow d'yer know?" asked Carol.

"She told me. She said, *Jeff you handsome brute. If you ever want to sink that gorgeous monster into my untouched well, feel free.*"

"Bollocks!"

"Said she'd suck them 'til they shrank."

"See what yer done now, Cas. He never talked like that before you come 'ere."

"So, he's got an education now. Yer should be proud."

"Git!"

"Slut!"

"Tart!"

"Bitch!"

"Ladies please. Not again. Let's go Plymouth an' see Gus."

"'Ere Jeff. This geezer Gus. He's not into pain as well is he?" Carol asked squirming in her seat.

Jeff smiled. "I'm not certain. All I can say is he was the most caned fifth former at Hemsworth. Some said he wanted to be remembered and could not achieve that accolade either athletically or academically. Others believed he simply liked it."

"Oh Gawd! Better pack the smackers as well then. The trouble is I'm getting' to like it too much."

Lisa had said very little on the journey down from Honiton. An overturned articulated lorry at Ashburton had held them up for over an hour. As Cork neared Launceston on the A388 he felt an urgent need for a shit. What to do with the girl, though? She would leg it the second his back was turned.

"Lisa." Cork broke the silence. "Do you enjoy your pathetic existence?"

"Eh?" Words of more than one syllable confused her.

"I'll re-phrase. Do you like living?"

"Oh no." She began to sob. "Y..you…ain't…g..gonna…k..kill…me…are… you?

"I didn't say that did I? You stupid bitch."

"What then?" Her crying ceased.

"Answer the fucking question. Do..you..like...living?"

"Yes."

"Thank God! Simple enough question wasn't it?"

"You're bloody rotten you are. I don't deserve to be treated like this…"

"SHUT UP!"

Silence reigned once more. Cork smouldered. He gained control once more and continued. "Are you hungry?"

"Yes."

"Are you thirsty?"

"Yes."

"Do you need to visit the toilet?"

"Not half."

"Right. I shall explain matters carefully. Listen to what I say. Obey and you shall live to slap your boyfriends face. I am going to stop off at a pub. I shall buy us both a meal and a drink. You can visit the toilet. We shall be father and daughter. You will smile. You will be happy. You will not draw attention to us. If you try anything at all I will kill you, with my bare hands if necessary. If you run I shall find you and I will take your miserable, wretched life. Not only that I will shoot anybody else that gets in my way. I will murder as a matter of course the youngest child I see. If you want that to happen then fuck with me. I have to admit I made a mistake picking you up. I should have resisted the temptation, got on with the job in hand. I didn't. I'm sorry I have to put you through this. Understand I cannot let you go yet. I cannot risk you running to the police. So I'm afraid you will have to bear with me a little longer. When I have caught up with those tarts I will let you go. I have no axe to grind with you. I shall not kill you unless you let me down. When I escaped the authorities I was on my way to a mad house, you see I am certified insane. I was on my way from Dartmoor to Broadmoor when as luck would have it I managed to evade my guards."

"Cork!" Lisa suddenly spluttered.

"That's right. John Cork. How do you know of me?"

"You're splashed all over this morning's papers. You owned a ship once."

"The Pegasus."

"And you're an ex-copper."

"Indeed."

"You done some awful things to people didn't you?"

"That has been said."

"And you reckon you'll let me go after I've witnessed you murder who ever it is you are after?"

"I have no reason to kill you girl. I am already a fugitive. Once my business is done I shall disappear, permanently. I have no reason to fear you."

"If you say so."

"You'll behave yourself then?"

"Got no bloody choice have I?"

By the time Cork pulled into the Horse and Groom's car park his situation was desperate. Cheeks squeezed he walked stiffly to the bar, Lisa holding his hand. He didn't see, couldn't see in the dark, the silver Mercedes containing Jeff, Suzanne and Carol whisper past on their way to Plymouth.

Inside Cork led Lisa to the loos. "Go do whatever you have to, but wash your face. Your Mascara has run. And don't come out until I knock three times. Savvy?"

Lisa nodded and darted through the sprung door.

She waited for his rap, not daring to disobey. The toilet was devoid of human life. She had washed then lit a cigarette, hands shaking. God! What a mess! She would get Phil for this if she survived. If the bastard hadn't dumped her then she would be comfortable in front of the TV, not waiting to see if mister psycho Cork would let her see another day. If only!

She should not have thrown Colin in Phil's face. All right the arrogant pig had pushed her relentlessly, always saying what a good mate Colin was and how he owed him a favour or two. Of how he had to go to Corfu with him. Did she really have to tell him Colin had been inside her knickers only the day before?

Of course Phil hadn't believed her. His best mate wouldn't betray him. But there again Colin was a man and men tried it on.

Three taps on the door. Lisa straightened her skirt, checked her face in the mirror and joined Cork for lunch.

What a different man. He was charming, humorous, even downright funny at times and generous. She was unaware it was somebody else's money, somebody else's suit and somebody else's motor.

Lisa eat what she wanted and drank her choice, her glass always full. She left the Horse and Groom a tipsy young woman, caring a lot less than when she had entered.

By the time Cork reached Bridge House on the outskirts of Tregadillet, Jane the housekeeper had arrived and taken up temporary residence. Had she known her future she would have stayed at home.

Jane, alone in the world apart from her cat, that temporarily in the care of a neighbour, was a good looking, unused woman for her age. Of average height and slim build she had born the years well. Shoulder length dark brown hair curled inward at the neck, a source of constant irritation as the ends continuously tickled her chin. Deep brown intelligent eyes looked out on a world devoid of love and children, although that had never caused her bitterness, a gentle conscientious woman who had loved and lost, to never love again.

Jane had fallen for a seaman when living in Plymouth some twenty years before. The wedding set she made the arrangements and invited the guests. Her man never returned, lost to the sea. Mountainous waves and hurricane force winds had taken him, his crew mates and the deep sea trawler, to Davy Jones Locker.

She had refrained from pre-marital sex for reasons of her upbringing. That perhaps was her only regret in life. Perhaps God willing she may have mothered his child. At least then she would have retained a part of him.

Jane was immediately suspicious of the knock on the door. It was too late; there were no expected guests. Cautiously she called from behind the door. "Who is it?"

"Detective sergeant Wilson and DC Atley to see Miss Carol Widney. We have some bad news I'm afraid."

Jane immediately opened the door. Faced with Cork and Lisa her suspicions turned to fear. "You don't look like the police," she chanced, scrutinising Lisa's dress.

"Quite right to suspect madam. We are directly from vice operations. The only unit currently available I'm afraid. You see Miss Atley portrays a prostitute and I the pimp."

"I see. Exciting work is it?"

"No ma'am, boring most of the time, although it does have its moments. Now is Miss Widney at home?"

"I'm sorry, the young lady in question, Carol isn't it? I've never actually met her but if she were here she would have gone with young Master Bridges I assume. He is away for a few days with his wife to be."

"Miss Dixon?"

"Yes."

"It is imperative I find Miss Widney. A young man has been found dead in her flat."

"Oh good grief! Poor thing. However did you trace her here?"

"She left a forwarding address."

"How considerate."

"Their whereabouts?"

"Plymouth."

"An address?"

"May I see your warrant card officer, only we cannot be too careful these days. I mean that awful Cork is still on the run isn't he? I've heard he has a terrible hatred for Miss Dixon's friend."

"Cork? Who's he?"

"A long story. But he is a dangerous lunatic. One can't be too careful you know." She gazed expectantly. "Your card sergeant?"

"Oh dear. You really should have just provided the address," Cork said pulling the revolver from his jacket pocket. "Now we have to do it the hard way. John Cork my dear. Dangerous lunatic."

"I knew, I just knew it." Jane tried to slam the door but Cork had his ex-coppers boot wedged before she could.

Jane grabbed the hall phone. Cork tore it from her grasp. Replacing it he said. "Don't be stupid. Now we have some talking to do. You can make your life easy or not. Up to you. You'll tell me what I want to know sooner or later, sooner if you have any sense in that pretty head."

With a quaver in her voice and trying to sound confident, Jane replied. "I'll not tell you anything. Look at you. Just look. You're like Bonnie and Clyde the pair of you. I suppose this young...." She gave Lisa a contemptuous look. "Trollop is your moll."

Cork laughed. Drawing a cigarette from its pack he lit it.

"Don't smoke in here please," Jane told him curtly.

Cork smiled and puffed on the tobacco. "Lisa tell this woman why you are with me. No. On second thoughts I shall. I do so hate formalities. Your name?"

"Miss Willett."

"Oh come now. Christian name, that is if you are one. First name if you're not."

She somehow knew not to aggravate him. He smelt psycho first class. "Jane," she informed him.

"That's so much better don't you think? Friendly you see. Almost intimate. I like intimacy. Now Miss Jane Willett, this young woman is Lisa. Lisa is on the run from a mental hospital. Oh she hasn't done any harm to anybody, not yet.

She has been experiencing delusions you see Jane." He drew slowly on the cigarette, then expertly blew a smoke ring. "She believes she is the descendant of the Marquis De Sade. She has these urges, don't you Lisa?"

Lisa by then completely in his thrall and wishing only to live, nodded.

"She longs to be let loose. To tender exquisite pain. If you do not tell me what I want to know, you will leave me no alternative but to let her play with you."

Jane stared aghast, between the devil and the deep blue sea it seemed. Be tortured or give information which could lead to someone's loss of life.

"Do your worst you evil swine," she spat.

"Rest assured Jane I shall. But first we should check the house. Maybe. Just maybe you are lying. Maybe the tarts are holed up warm and snug in a bed somewhere. Shall we go see."

Jane grudgingly led them from room to room, all devoid of human life, until finally they reached the locked door of Jeff's special den.

"Hiding in here are they?" Cork inquired, suspicious.

"I told you they have gone away. I don't know why this door is locked."

Jane leapt as Cork's boot kicked it, the lock no use against his professional boot.

"Come out, come out, wherever you are," Cork called into the black silence.

"Why won't you listen? There is nobody else in this house."

"So you said Jane. So you said."

Cork's hand felt for a light switch, successful the room abruptly illuminated. Gormless he stared in disbelief. He not the only one.

"Good God!" Jane exclaimed, her jaw dropping. "All this time........I never had an inkling."

With the women ushered in, the fugitive from the asylum closed the door. "Hell sent I should say," he remarked pointedly. "Seems like the tarts have been holding out on me. To think, they probably enjoyed my attentions. Most interesting." Cork picked up a cane laying on a bench and idly swished it. "What think you of your friends now Jane?"

"Mine is not to judge," she answered defensively, considering where her next job might lie.

Cold grey eyes studied her face from beneath silvered bushy brows. A wry smile played on thin lips. A glint to his eye he commended. "Loyalty is admirable Jane. But loyalty to perverts, now come woman you can see what they get up to. You seriously wish to protect such deviants. God only knows what else they........"

"That's right God knows and he shall judge. Not you or I. And you're a fine one to talk, I've read of your carryings on."

"Deary me, was it such an explicit article? Such fame and I missed it. Perhaps Jane. Perhaps you also are party to their games. Maybe you care for a bit of the old bum slash yourself."

"How dare you! You....you disgusting foul mouthed animal. I'll........"

"Enough." His mood changed radically. "Where are the tarts? Where Jane?"

"I told you, Plymouth." Fear etched her face. "That's all I........"

"Liar! Iniquitous devious bitch! You know damn well where they are. Tell me or I shall bring the devil himself to see you."

"You are the devil, or the devil's disciple."

"You better believe it babe."

"You touch me and……"

"Touch you! I'll flay you alive." The thunderous expression faded as quickly as it had settled. "Do I really have to Jane? You'll tell me what I want to know soon enough. Do you really want me to hurt you?"

The middle aged woman, tight lipped said nothing.

"So be it." The cane flashed, slicing her upper arm. As she instinctively reached to soothe the smart, Cork threw the rod aside. His strong hand seized her by the throat. He lifted her effortlessly, fingers digging painfully into her flesh. "Now your education begins," he promised.

Cork carried her thus, her own hands ineffectually tearing at his forearm, her legs bucking and kicking. She could breathe, but only just. A slow paralysis crept into her convulsive body.

Dumped unceremoniously on a wooden structure, the fiend's hand still about her throat his face came close to hers. His complexion rough, heated, the eyes mad, staring, cold and heartless he hissed. "Now Jane. Sweet Jane." Veins stood proud about the temples, spittle daubed his chin, he continued, his voice hoarse with rage. "You do exactly as I tell you or I shall break that delicate upturned nose of yours. Now take off that charity shop reject, then unbutton your blouse." He released her, his presence still threatening.

Slowly the baggy woollen garment, the target of his ridicule, fell from her shoulders. Trembling fingers sought the fastenings of the blouse. Faltering, she grudgingly released the buttons one by one, stopping dead as Cork suddenly bellowed.

"LISA!" Without so much as a glance away from Jane, he continued quietly. "Where do you think you were going sweetie pie. Remember, I still have a lead appetiser for that yet unblemished belly of yours. It takes a long time to die that way Lisa."

She ceased her furtive backward shuffle. "Weren't going nowhere, honest Mister Cork."

"I know you weren't Lisa. Now come stand opposite me. You can study the artful caress of rattan on flesh. Watch carefully least you become careless.

Do proceed Jane. Off with the blouse now woman. Let us enjoy your choice of underwear."

The blouse fell to join the cardigan. Cork eyed the white linen full cup brassiere covering Jane's virgin bosom. "As I suspected," he chided. "I suppose you have full length bloomers beneath the tweed," he sniggered.

Jane found her tongue once more. "What I chose as suitable and fitting has nothing to do with you. You may scoff in your trivial sarcastic manner, but rest assured I shall laugh last when they bang your cell door shut for all time."

"Will you Jane? Do you suppose you will be around to see that day?"

What little colour Jane had evaporated. "You intend to murder me?"

"No sweet Jane. No of course not. But you'll be long dead of old age before they catch up with me."

"Arrogance will be your downfall Cork. You'll pay the price one way or the other."

"Bra off Jane. Let me see the state of your droop."

The housekeeper shook her head. "No more. I'll strip no more. You want, you take it."

Cork smiled. "Lisa, undo the baggage's bra."

Lisa did, too frightened not to. Cork slipped two fingers between the cups and pulled the item free.

"Oh my, such sweet dainty morsels," he remarked crudely on seeing her bosom bared.

"What surprising delicacies. Can't you just feel the whip cutting them, eh Jane?"

The fissure in her mettle began to widen. "You wouldn't," she stammered.

"Oh I would. I truly would Jane. And I'd enjoy doing it. Please Jane don't doubt me for I have nothing to lose do I? I am already sentenced to be detained on her Majesty's pleasure indefinitely. What more can the authorities do? Hang me?"

"Oh that they would. I would love to see you swing," Jane retorted.

"And I you. Dance on the end of a rope. Now that's something new. I've already shot one, why not hang one? Eh?"

"Craven, bullying threats. Do you believe I will tell you anything now?"

"Mmmmh. Face down Jane. Lay face down. You do not know what you are sitting on do you?"

"What?"

"A rack. I am going to make you taller. Would you like to grow some? I understand disjointing limbs is very painful indeed."

Figure 1 Chapter 9 Mates is Mates

9-Mates is Mates, Or is they?

Jeff brought the BMW series seven to a halt outside a small cottage on the seaward side of Plymouth; the sports car then dispensed with. Suzanne had complained that the two seater was of no use to a family and had experienced difficulty in extricating her bulk from the car's cramped compartment.

A fresh faced young man answered the door to them. Slim of build, a freckled complexion encompassed intelligent, deep set blue eyes. A crop of tight ginger curls perched ludicrously atop an otherwise shaven plate.

"Jeff. Suzanne," he cried excitedly. "And, and who is this?" he asked his smile broadening.

"Carol," the blond quickly answered.

The young man's hand darted to grab Carol's. Shaking it vigorously he babbled. "Ever so pleased to meet you."

"Yeah, an' you." Carol stared down on the meeting of limbs as he continued his energetic greeting. "Is yer gonna shake it off? Or is yer tryin' to pump me up?" she asked, sarcastic.

"Oh sorry," he said letting the hand go. "It's just you're my first visitors in weeks and as you can see I'm a touch overcome."

The detached house was cramped. An old seaman's abode it offered two up and two down. A small cluttered sitting room, not particularly well kept contained rows of books stacked precariously on bowing shelves. That room fronted a tiny shabby kitchen. Two bedrooms and a bathroom occupied the space upstairs.

Gus cleared debris from the two seater settee and solitary armchair, inviting his guests to seat themselves on the battered relics.

"Coffee? Or something stronger?" he inquired.

"Coffee's fine by me," Jeff answered, the girls nodded accordingly. Gus disappeared into the kitchen.

"Well," said Carol sighing. "Your mate's pleasant enough." Not struck by the man's lack of good looks, that was all she could find in herself to say.

Jeff sat himself beside Carol. "He's a really decent bloke Cas. He's shy that's all. I don't think he has ever had a girlfriend. Can't you pretend? You know act like you fancy him?"

"One thing I don't do Jeff. Supposin' he gets the wrong idea? I tell yer now I ain't sleepin' wiv 'im cos he's your mate. I ain't no fuckin' charity yer knows."

"No. I never said kip with him. Just bolster his confidence that's all."

"'Ow many bedrooms 'ere Jeff?" Carol asked suspicious.

"Er, two." The lad admitted.

"Looks like yer sleeps wiv yer mate then don't it? You an' me cuddles time Sooze."

Suzannes face lit up.

"Don't get the wrong idea Cas," Jeff blurted apologetically. "I never had any devious intentions, honest."

"No. I don't suppose yer did," she agreed. "Just men bein' thick I suppose."

Gus returned, a tray of coffee and sandwiches in hand. They talked, chatted over new and old times. The beers and vodka bottle made an appearance. They drank, excepting Suzanne who took her pregnancy very seriously.

Hours ticked by and by late evening inhibitions were somewhat suppressed.

"Tell me Gus, because I've always wanted to know," Jeff began, the beer having lowered his inhibitions. "Why were you the most caned in our year?"

"Bad bugger I suppose," Gus returned.

"What was the worst yer got?" asked Carol, she also half pissed.

"Oh nine, from Old Peculiar."

"Old Peculiar?" Suzanne questioned laughing.

"Yeah. Mister Cuthbertson. He were weird."

"Nine of what?" Carol pressed.

"Oh the cane. On my underpants, trousers around my ankles. I tell you I felt that for days after."

"What yer do then?" Carol asked slinging another vodka and orange down the chute.

"I let his bike tyres down."

"Is that all?"

"After I had brazed the chain to the sprocket."

"Why d'yer do that?" Carol asked choking on another drink.

"Because he was a prat."

"Okay then," Jeff pressed. "What's the best whacking you had?"

Without consideration, the alcohol having dulled his acumen, Gus answered. "Oh that's easy. Miss Hardcastle and her skipping rope."

"What happened then?" Jeff asked pursuing the tale.

"She caught me looking through the keyhole of the door to the girl's changing rooms."

"Yer little pervy," squealed Carol.

"Yer never told me yer wents to a mixed school Jeff." Suzie chided

"It was and it wasn't. Both sexes attended in separate classes, separate recreation areas. We shared the gymnasium with individual changing rooms, both leading out into the gym."

"Anyway," Gus persevered. "It was a waste of time because I couldn't see anything. Next I hear Miss Hardcastle bawling at me. 'You disgusting brat. How dare you? How dare you? You, you peeping Tom.' I was ordered to shower and not to dress but to await her pleasure in the buff. She had decided that a fair and fitting prelude to my chastisement, due to my having attempted to see her girls in that state.

Anyway she made me wait, to dwell on what she would do. Now Miss Hardcastle was a cracker, an absolute beaut. To be whacked by her was a privilege. To be thrashed on the bare bum by her was the pinnacle.

She eventually appeared, still wearing her sports gear. A tight vest, and I swear she had no bra on, gorgeous bristols. A short pleated skirt and socks. She sent my heart a racing I can tell you.

'Bend over the bar,' she instructed holding a doubled skipping rope in her hand. The bar being the chromed construction fencing in the showers. I duly doubled for her. God did she lash my arse with that rope. Twelve good stripes she gave me.

I stood up and unfortunately that wasn't all that was stood up. She took one look at my stiff and blushing in anger she grabbed me by the hair and forced me back over. What a whipping I got. I lost count. She laid into my backside and thighs with a vengeance. I was red raw by the time she finished.

Thankfully my pecker was down by the time she had finished, but she warned me that if she caught me anywhere near that door again I'd feel the cane on my bare behind." Gus grinned. "I tried but she never seemed to be about at the right moment after that."

"You enjoyed that hiding then?" Jeff asked smiling.

"Yeah." Gus stared at his feet, his face burning with embarrassment. "Bad isn't it?"

"No Gus. Not bad, merely different."

"But I'm weird aren't I? To enjoy pain that is."

"No Gus. We're all the same," Jeff admitted.

The lad's eyes widened. "What all three of you?"

"Yes Gus." Jeff glanced at a hushed Carol. "Show him your bum Cas."

"Bugger off. You show him yours."

"Okay." Jeff stood up, tottered a few steps and downed his strides, his backside still demonstrating the marks of the birch.

"I say," Gus stammered. "Well I'll be. I thought I was on my own."

"Not so me old mate. I often wondered if you were inclined."

"It's been a long time. School was the last time. In fact Carol you do look a bit like Miss Hardcastle." His voice fell to a whisper. "A real cracker."

Carol hic-cupped. "Does yer want yer bum smacked then Gus?"

His face lit up. "Cor, would you?"

"Got a rope?"

"I've got a cane," he replied obviously excited.

"Go get it then."

"Thanks Cas," Jeff said once Gus was gone.

"S'alright. I ain't gonna fuck 'im, only whack 'is arse," she slurred.

"I warned you before you dirty little git what would 'appen if I caught yer at that door again. Didn't I?" Carol berated, pretending to be the idolised Miss Hardcastle.

"Now yer bad bugger yer can drop yer trousers an' pants an' bend over, cos I'm gonna welt yer bare botty like I said I would." Carol swayed as she spat the words at an excited, cowed Gus.

Gus turned and wrestled with his waistband buttons. The zip descended as did his lower garments. He bent touching his toes, his meatless derriere on offer.

Carol yanked up the tail of his shirt fully exposing the scant buttocks. "Gawd yer don't carry much meat d'yer Gus?" she declared. "Six of the best yer pervert."

Jeff and Suzanne sat cuddling, watching the exhibition unfold. Carol levelled the cane, withdrew it to over her shoulder then dealt the skinny cheeks a slice of hell. Gus heard the hiss of parted air, the slap of rod on flesh, then felt the incredible smart as the rattan charged its toll.

He leapt with the connection, a searing fire ripping through his lower buttocks. His witnesses watched enthralled.

As the stroke bore fruit, a thin line of scarlet, Carol struck again. The cheeks quivered to her attendance, the rod cavorting upon his whipped flesh. A strangled cry escaped his dry mouth.

A third crippled, raising a message of suffering mid arse. Gus swore.

A fourth hit still higher, three distinct tramlines grew in strength beneath.

The fifth neared the summit.

The sixth atop the flushing rear. Gus straightened bringing his trousers up with him.

"Oy!" Carol snapped. "Not so fast matey. I seem to remember yer 'ad a bit of trouble with a certain prominence last time. Turn around yer little sod an' let me see."

His face redder than his behind Gus complied. It was Carol's turn for a surprise, for there saluting her stood eight and a half inches of the thickest cock she'd ever seen.

"Good Gawd buster!" she wheezed. "Yer prick don't take after the rest of yer do it?"

Gus smiled nervously. "Sorry," he whispered.

"Don't apologise matey. Yer should be proud of a tool like that." She stared stupidly at the monster. "Cos what it do mean is I'm gonna have to whip yer arse some more. Can't have a display like that yer knows. Bend over again yer dirty little, er per'aps not so little pervy."

Still coloured, his experience with the opposite sex non-existent, Gus bent back over.

Carol gave him another six belters, slashing his tiny butt unsparingly, marking him cruelly. Gus revelled in the barbaric abuse, even through the mass of nerves he suffered.

Up he came again, this time leaving his trousers around his ankles. "You've been taking lessons off of Old Peculiar haven't you?" he asked Carol, frantically rubbing his bum.

"Ain't done no good 'as it?" Carol gazed wistfully at his king sized member.

"Are you going to cane me some more?" Gus asked a touch worried, his butt still on fire.

The trouble with Carol was although she didn't fancy Gus one iota, she longed for that ultra thick, lengthy piece with a fervour.

She looked up at Gus. "'Ow's yer arse?" she asked mischievously.

"I bet yer this 'ardcastle tart never done this to yer." She placed both of her small hands about his considerable circumference and held him tight.

"N…n…no," he managed.

She knelt. "An' I bet she never done this either." Her lips kissed his dome. A hand wandered to his nuts and fondled.

"N...n...n...n...no sh..sh..she didn't," he gasped.

"Or this." Carol pulled back the foreskin. "'Ow about this." Gus watched his end disappear into the warm confines of Carol's mouth, her lips stretched so tight about him.

"Oh God!" Gus breathed. "Oh dear, dear God Almighty!" His cock spasmed and years of pent up frustrations pumped energetically, the hot seed filling her orifice.

"Sorry," he cried, dragging the goliath from her warm embrace.

"No worries," Carol returned, wiping her mouth. "We'll see if he won't come back up again eh?"

"Carol."

"Yeah."

"I'm a virgin."

"I had guessed. The thing is do you want to stay a virgin?" she enquired releasing a blouse button.

"Oh no, no I want to do it. Really I do. I just never thought it would happen with such a beautiful woman. In fact I never thought it would happen at all."

"Yer throws yer dice and takes yer chance." Carol fully unfastened the shirt, then descending on the trembling young man she cupped a hand behind his head and kissed him, seducing, reducing his will power to nothing.

Stepping away slightly she smiled and then pulled his face to her ample cleavage, pressing his hot features between her bosom. She held him there stroking the curly ginger bob, his arms hung limp by his sides.

Suzanne, the urge building released Jeff's phallus and descended on him, sucking and gorging herself. Jeff pulled up her dress and sank his hand beneath her skimp briefs, fondling her rump.

Gus surfaced his countenance scarlet, to see his friend, eyes closed, his prick firmly planted in Suzie's open mouth and her buttocks barely covered by the strip of black material. His ardour began to reform.

Carol unbuttoned Gus' shirt, her hand seeking beneath, caressing, touching, soothing. Still he refrained from an intimacy, terrified of error.

His shirt slid to the floor, followed by Carol's. "Undo me bra then Gus. Fill yer 'ands. The only stiff I wanna see is the one between yer legs."

He fumbled, fought, his shaking hands unable to comprehend the twin catches of her harness. Exasperated Carol did it for him. Then provocatively she slid the straps down her arms and eased the brassiere clear of her breasts. The gorgeous orbs sprang free, the welts from the master clearly visible.

"You've been whipped," he gasped amazed.

"Yeah an' 'ow! Me tits, me bum and me..." She slid a hand down between her legs.

"No!"

"Oh yeah. Sweet bloody ecstasy. Per'aps I might do that enormous cock of yours sometime." Her hand grasped it, the life flooding back.

Carol turned about and raised her arms above her head. "All yours," she invited. Gus circumnavigated her ribs and took a mammary in each hand. Gently he squeezed, his first touch of female breast. Carol sensed his hardness pressing to her buttocks, anticipating its first intrusion.

"Now Gus lift me skirt and put yer 'ands inside me knickers, 'andle me cheeks."

With thumping heart he obliged. And as he sank so seductively within he watched Suzie take off her dress and panties and lower herself onto Jeff's waiting face. His ticker threatened to explode.

"D'yer want some of that?" Carol asked, noting the distraction. "Cos I do chummy."

"Yeah, whatever," Gus agreed.

He lay down and observed Carol remove the skirt and scant underwear. Naked she knelt astride him gazing down. "'Appy?" she asked.

"In heaven," he replied.

"D'yer know what's expected of yer?"

"Er, not really Cas."

"Yer knows what a pussy is?"

"Yeah, course."

"Does yer know how to pussy lick?"

Gus turned a little green. "Sorry Cas, I'll probably not be very good at it."

"Course yer will. When I puts mine to yer gob, yer licks all 'round it. Don't yer worry none, it's clean. Then Gus, yer parts me pussy lips, not that I've got any, an' yer runs yer tongue all around just inside. Just 'ere." She indicated the fore of the slit. "This is me clit. A little bobble, yer'll feel it. Yer licks it until it can't get no bigger. Yer can stick yer tongue right up me fanny. In fact yer can licks what yer likes down there.

An' while yer's working me 'ole to a frenzy, yer feels me bits an' pieces. Yer knows me tits, nipples an' arse. Play wiv me Gus. Get me all turned on an' I'll fuck yer silly after."

"Sounds good," he whispered, an onslaught of nerves stealing his voice.

Carol offered her bush. She slid forward, he so aware of her bum cheeks draped to his clavicles.

Tentatively he touched, the labia soft to his caress. He filled his hands with her firm buttocks, squeezing the plumpness. His tongue dipped between the velvet folds, the briny taste sharp to his buds.

Shy and not at all sure of himself he found the cunnilingus a trial. The thought of her juices mixing in his mouth brought a lump to his throat. But he wanted to have her more than anything. Carol epitomised the tart. A big hearted, extremely attractive tart, but a tart all the same. He wanted the trophy to place on his mantelpiece.

After what seemed an eternity of delving that saturated gorge she gasped and pulled away from him. He glanced across the room to see Jeff hammering away at Suzie's behind, his stem firmly immersed in her organ.

No gentle lead in for Gus. No ignorant foreplay. No dancing about the subject. No frustrating refusals, anticipation or waiting. No, an orgy for losing his virginity. What a night!

"Yer ready sunshine for the 'ole 'og?"

Gus nodded.

"Any preference?"

"I don't mind. Really I don't."

"Me on top? You on top? From behind likes them over there? Or something real kinky?"

"Kinky sounds interesting."

"If yer is gonna do it then do it in its extreme eh? 'Ow about I lays on the sofa next to Suzie wiv me legs pulled right back?"

"Can we do it the same way as them? Next to them?"

"Yeah course, if that's yer heart's desire. Come on lover boy."

What a sight befell his innocent eyes. Carol's rounded welted arse before him, the pleasant division of her crotch waiting his pleasure. Jeff's stiff stretching Suzie's hole, her bum quivering to the lad's thrusts, her dangling breasts gyrating with the constant jostling, both oblivious to anything or anybody.

With his prick about to explode Gus attempted an entry. He tried unsuccessfully to ram it home. Carol's fingers appeared between her legs and she parted her difference for him. He sank blissfully into her, his girth stretching her admirably. He grasped her buttocks as he pressed his message home, taking Carol to the limit.

She caught hold of the cushion she lay on, her face a picture of intensity. Gus's prick filled her completely. She took his all, eight and a half inches of rampant phallus; him not stopping until his groin met her plump cheeks.

She gasped in reply to his thrusts, a frown of concentration twisting her pretty features. Gus wasn't long. His experience telling, he shot his seed prematurely, withdrawing to lay fully satisfied on the floor. Jeff still pumped away at Suzie.

Carol checked out the prostrate figure with misgivings, then said casually to Jeff. "When yer done there mate finish us off will yer."

Suzie sighed and relaxed. Jeff pulled free, side stepped and plummeted into Carol, bringing her off and releasing his load.

"I don't believe this," Gus groaned. "That's infidelity that is."

"Only if yer misses objects Gus. And she don't."

"Do you mean you, you know, with both of them?"

"Yeah. Want a turn at Suzie then?"

Gus flushed, embarrassed. "I don't think that's up to you."

Suzie's dreamy voice interrupted. "I don't mind Gus," she confirmed, her mind dwelling on his immense erection.

"I'll need a while. Excuse me, the bathroom." He was gone, his striped bare arse rushing through the door to the stairs.

"This has all the signs of becoming one filthy night," Suzie reflected.

"It's Gus's birthday tomorrow girls," Jeff disclosed. "What a pressie he's had."

Carol piped up. "We'll 'ave to make it a night to remember."

Jeff scowled. "You've changed your tune Cas. I thought you didn't fancy him?"

"I don't. But that prick is some'at else. If he can just learn to keep it in a bit, er longer I'll be quite 'appy."

"Give him time Cas," Jeff suggested.

Carol inspected her breasts and asked absently. "'Ow long before these marks go d'yer reckon?"

Jeff grinned. "Bothering you are they?"

"Nah, not really. I just likes to look me best, that's all."

"About a week and you'll be back to perfection."

Carol sucked her bottom lip, she looked furtively at Jeff. "Yer knows what I fancies Jeff,"

"What?"

"A double."

"Vodka?"

"Nah prick!"

"Double prick?"

"Yeah, both of yer at the same time."

"We wouldn't fit."

"Wanna bet. Anyway I wasn't thinking of them both up me pussy. Nah, I thought if Gus took that yer could tend me arse."

"If we oblige you, will you see to us?"

"I thought that was what I was offerin'"

"A blow job each first."

"D'yer reckon yer mate could manage me 'ole after I done that to 'im?"

"Don't bring him off then. Just take him to the edge."

"Difficult wiv 'im. He don't seem to 'ave no control."

"All right then bring us both off and we'll have you later."

"'Ere you two, what about me? I may be near ready to drop but I feel I'm bein' left out."

"Yeah okay Sooze." Jeff reached out and stoked her hair. "You give Gus a job and Cas me. Then we'll have Cas and you later."

"Yer can forget me bum hole. I ain't into that. I'll just settle for Gus. It is 'is beeday after all. Be my little gift. A furry pussy to swallow 'is snake."

Gus returned with no idea of the decisions made.

"Come and sit by Suzie," the brunette suggested. Gus tried to make himself comfortable, but Suzanne thrust her hand between his legs. "Come on boy part them thighs. Let Sooze rub some life back into yer."

Her fingers cupped his balls, while her free arm went about his neck and drew him to her teat. He suckled as a baby while she squeezed and manipulated his swelling.

"Well wench!" Jeff barked. "Why dost thou stand there idle when thou couldst be tending thy master's proud meat?"

"Yer what yer barmpot?"

"On thy knees servile harlot, unless thou wouldst care to taste the whip instead?"

"I think I've done enough tasting lately thank you. All the same sir, I'll have the sausage if yer don't mind."

As Carol dropped to her knees uncovering Jeff's glistening dome, so Suzie swooped on a euphoric Gus, her small mouth struggling to consume his circumference.

Gorged, massaged, suckled, licked, so the two young men entered a piece of heaven, both succumbing to the lavish attention laid upon their eager ends. Gus not wanting to presume allowed Suzie to do all the work. Jeff an old hand, took Carol by the hair and holding her he began to thrust, she quite willing to play the host.

Both worldly birds readily received the seed, cherishing the delivery to its last drop. Gus cradled a cushion, squeezing the pillow as his organ pumped, his cock pulsating. Suzie, her mouth full of rigid stem, gobbled him to the bitter end.

Jeff lay back in the armchair, a leg cocked over one arm, heedless of his brazen exposure. Carol removed a cigarette from its pack. "D'yer mind Gus?" she asked politely. He shook his head, still revelling in probably his best orgasm ever.

Nothing was said as Carol relaxed with her smoke. For some five minutes she reclined puffing a blue haze into the hot tense atmosphere. Finished she stubbed it out.

Jeff broke the silence. Critical he carped. "Not very good, were you girls?"

"Eh?" They returned as one.

"You weren't very good. That was one of the worst blow jobs ever. What say you Gus?"

"Mmmmmh," he uttered oblivious.

"See Gus isn't impressed either."

"You fuckin' cheeky sod!" Carol shrieked.

"Tsk! Tsk! Such language. Foul mouthed slut."

"You're on a fuckin' wind up ain't yer pig shite?"

"No Carol, I'm not. If you do something you should do it well. And if you don't you should be punished."

"Oh that's yer game is it? Fancy a bit of bum whack do yer?"

"I think Carol Widney you should get six strokes for incompetence."

"Oh yeah?"

"And Suzie six for hers."

"Yer can't whack a pregnant woman for Christ's sake!" Carol cried alarmed.

"Why not?"

"Cos it ain't done, that's why."

"Then perhaps you'll take hers for her?"

"Yer what?"

"Six from me and six from Gus."

Carol eyed Jeff up, her jaw set firm, a scowl settled on her face. "Don't yer ever 'ave enough?"

"Nope. Are you going to bend over or shall I make you whore?"

"Oh come on Bridges me bloody arse is like a road map already. Yer ain't serious? Yer can't be!"

Jeff rose from his seat. "Got any rope Gus?"

Carol knew that if she wound up bound it would be the worse for her. And a spanking before Gus and indeed by him did prove appealing.

"Oh all right." She surrendered, beginning to rise.

"No," Jeff corrected. "On second thoughts on your knees and elbows."

Carol warily complied.

"Now," he said picking up the cane. "Kiss the carpet. I want your bum thrust right up."

Down Carol went, thighs vertical, back dipped toward the floor, shoulders touching it. She presented the roundness of her behind, ready for a downward slice.

Gus rudely aroused sat abruptly, watchful, intent. Suzanne relaxed, a thrill driving through her groin. Carol waited expectantly, excited about being thrashed and before an audience.

Jeff lay the cane on his shoulder, clutching the end tightly. He eyed the target, then swiftly slashed the rattan downward. The rod whooshed, struck, branding a cheek with its brief visit. The end curved exquisitely to her form, licking down toward the hip joint.

Carol gasped.

Jeff deliberated. The welt ripened. The cane rent air for a second incursion, slapping noisily on her right buttock again, an inch or two below the first.

"Ow!" Carol squealed.

He bent to the third. A sweeping arc connecting painfully on the lower rump, smiting equally about the cleft.

"F…f…fuck!" escaped her.

The fourth, a similar assault, landed with a solid thump mid bottom.

"J…J…Jeff!" she shrieked questioning the strength of his delivery.

The lad stepped over her and laid the fifth to her left haunch, providing her with a six-inch welt on that buttock. The final stroke he dealt to both buttocks at the very top of the division.

Carol relaxed. She sank to the floor. "Gawd Jeff, that was bloody hard," she complained, her words falling on deaf ears.

"Your turn Gus. Any position you like and **don't** spare the rod."

"Any position?" Gus asked thrilled.

"Whatever mate." Jeff laughed.

"Okay. Get up Carol."

She clambered to her feet.

"Over by the wall. Feet there well apart." He indicated a spot three feet from the wall. "Now spread your arms, hands against the wall."

Gus viewed that tensed bum, then remembering Jeff's words provided Carol with an absolute stinger, carving a stripe over both cheeks.

"Bugger," she cursed.

He didn't wait, the cane returned an inch lower almost immediately, doubling her misery.

The third within six seconds. Carol clawed the wallpaper, biting hard on her bottom lip, her face screwed in torment.

The fourth whipped those rigid cheeks. She cried out.

The fifth and finally the sixth scored the bum thigh line.

She pushed from the wall, dancing wildly, her hands flying to those wounded mounds. She rubbed maniacally, lips pursed.

"You sod!" she yelled. "Gawd that don't 'alf fuckin' sting."

"It's meant to," Jeff admonished.

"I dunno why I keeps on agreein' to do this." She turned. "Just look at me arse."

"We are," came the lads reply. "We are."

She looked over a shoulder to see two Cheshire cats beaming, eyes fixed on her full, firm, striped rump.

"Dirty buggers," she snorted, her eyes narrowing.

Turned on by her ill-treatment she fondled Gus saying. "Lay on the floor then." He dropped to the carpet and reclined, his tent pole ready for action.

Carol straddled him, kneeling on all fours, his dick tucked to her pussy, her breasts swinging enticingly before his face. She grimaced as Jeff entered from behind, stretching her anus. Then she sank slowly on the veritable marrow.

As she descended so Jeff withdrew, as she rose so Jeff slid back in.

"Don't you wear it out girl," Suzie mocked, kneeling beside her man, his shaft in her clutches. "I'll 'elp yer mate. Make sure yer gives 'er it all." She swatted his clenched bare bum cheeks. He thrust.

Carol's hand went to her parted fanny lips, feeling the small labia tight about Gus's monster. She descended again, delighting in the stretch, drinking of the two fold intercourse. Something she had long hankered after.

Suzie continued to slap Jeff, no real force but enough to light up his rear end.

Gus tried to ignore the pendulous boobs, Carol's grunt and groans, the fact that his dick was being pounded by the constricting sex gorge. That somehow out of his line of sight Jeff was raging at her backside. That Suzie was in full view, also naked, swollen breasts quivering with her capers. And he tried to ignore the steady splat of hand on bare buttocks.

Gus did well considering he almost brought Carol off before shooting his wad deep within her crotch.

Saved by the heroic Jeff once more; when Carol ceased to go down, the action pointless as there was nothing to fall upon, the blond lad switched from rectum to pussy, pausing only to whip off his sheath.

He took her to orgasm with Gus still beneath, still fascinated by her swinging boobs.

Poor Gus still had to face Suzanne. There was no way she was letting the lad off.

An hour later and Gus's ardour looking like having collapsed, Suzie held the limpness between finger and thumb eyeing it contemptuously. "Only one thing to do," she declared. "Over me knee!"

"What knee?" Carol asked sarcastically. "Yer're all belly girl. There ain't no lap."

"All right then. Over your knees Cas."

Suzie squatted knees up legs apart leaning on the armrest of the settee. As Gus lay over Carol's lap, Suzie received his head between those soft limbs. Then she clamped her thighs about his face.

Carol spanked, slapped each buttock individually, the cheeks quickly colouring. Suzie held him breathless, his face millimetres from her bush.

As the hummocks commenced to glow so the phallus began to grow, pressing indelicately into Carol's thigh.

"I think he's ready Sooze," Carol casually informed her friend.

"So?"

"So do you want 'is piece now?"

"I'm rather enjoyin' watchin' 'is bum smacked actually."

"You're getting' dead sadistic you is gel," Carol commented contining to rain sharp blows to those sore dunes.

"I knows. It's me 'ormones Cas. Makes me right bitchy they do."

"Me arm's achin' Sooze."

"So's 'is bum gel. A couple more minutes eh? Looked yer missed a bit. It ain't as red as the rest."

"You'll be red in a minute."

"Yer can't hit a pregnant bird. Yer said it yerself."

"Can't cane I said. I can smack yer bum though."

"Yer can try yer silly cow."

Jeff listened, a broad grin splitting his face. He knew the signs and what would happen next.

"Get up Gus," Carol barked, staring hard at Sooze.

"I 'an't," came his muffled reply.

"Let 'is 'ead go or it'll be the worse for you."

Suzanne did, immediately clutching her abdomen. Gus rolled to the floor, out of harm's way. Jeff advanced and Carol crawled forward staring at the woman's swollen belly.

"What is it Sooze?" Carol pleaded, trying to look up into the girl's down turned face.

Suzie moved fast, her fists grabbing the blond's locks. She dragged her down and to one side crying out. "This dopey." As Carol half slid from the settee her butt came within reach. Suzie's hand flashed down smacking Carol's backside with gusto.

"I don't." SLAP! "knows." SLAP! "why's." SLAP! "yer." SLAP! "keeps." SLAP! "tryin'." SLAP! "to." SLAP! "get." SLAP! "the." SLAP! "better." SLAP! "of." SLAP! "me." SLAP!

"Yer." SLAP! "knows." SLAP! "I'm." SLAP! "smarter." SLAP! "than." SLAP! "you." SLAP! "Dim." SLAP! "cow!" SLAP!

She took hold of Carol's calves and tossed that half from her lap.

Carol stood, appearing chaste, feeling the heat in her buttocks. "That weren't fair," she complained. "That were underhanded."

Suzie laughed. "Yeah, weren't it just."

"When you've 'ad that kid. An' this is a promise. I'm gonna strap your fat backside black an' bloody blue. You sees if I don't."

"Yer can try kiddo, but yer'd better get yourself a brain transplant first. If yer wants to get the better that is."

"At least I ain't sneaky."

"No you ain't gel, just thick."

"Cas," Jeff whispered.

"What!"

"Whatever you're thinking of doing please don't. Think of Zac."

"Yeah I am."

Carol glanced at Gus still sitting on the floor. His erection stood clear of his legs. She stepped aside him. She pushed him over. She turned her back to his surprised stare and sank on his stiff.

Gus lay mesmerised as her strong thighs propelled her up and down on his piece.

"Hey yer cow! That's my cock!" Suzie shouted, perhaps a might too loudly.

"Was your cock," Carol corrected.

"You'll wank him out yer slime bag," Suzie protested."

"Oh Sooze, what a fuckin' shame."

"I don't believe you, yer greedy cow!"

"It's nice Sooze. All thick and hard. It really grabs the spot that matters. Just feeling his almighty stiff in yer. Oooooh Gawd it's bliss. Pity yer ain't 'ad the pleasure. Ain't it Sooze?"

"If I weren't so big I'd knock the shit out'a yer."

Carol continued to ride the monster, Gus partaking of the pleasure of her rising and sinking flushed arse.

"Shame ain't it cocky? Talking of cocky, don't yer just wish yer were jockeyin' this one?"

"'Ow many does that make now tart?"

"Three. Jealous bitch."

"No not just wiv Gus. I means all tolled. 'Ow many different dicks 'as yer 'ad up yer?"

"Who's countin'?"

"Must be getting' on for a couple 'undred I reckon."

Gus frowned.

"Nearer three 'undred I wouldn't wonder," Carol elaborated.

Jeff laughed.

"Yer ought a go for the records gel. Most fucked pussy in England."

"Most fucked in Europe yer means."

Gus scowled.

"Gawd yer've 'ad some meat in there an' that's with out the word of a lie."

"All kinds Sooze. Blacks; yellows; Scots; Welsh; Degos, all kinds."

"That's it!" Gus snapped, pushing Carol off. "God knows what you're carrying. And to think I haven't used a condom."

"I'd soak it in disinfectant if I was you," advised Suzie, stifling the giggles.

"Why didn't you tell me Jeff? You may not be fussy but I bloody well am!"

"It's a wind up Gus. These two are always at it."

"Yeah that's right Gus," Suzanne confirmed. "Cas is a virgin, ain't yer blondie?"

Angry at Gus's reaction Carol sided with her mate. "Yeah Gus, you're the very first. I never 'ad a prick up me until you."

Suzie lost control; she started to giggle at Carol's innuendo. That reaction quickly followed by Carol.

"I don't believe you," Gus spat angrily climbing into his underpants.

"True Gus, you're a total prick!" Carol opined.

"Charming! Just because I don't want a well laid whore fucking me, I'm a prick."

Jeff frowned. "Mind your mouth Gus, Cas is no whore."

"That's right," Suzie added. "She ain't never been paid a penny."

"What are you? I've heard about nymphomaniacs," Gus stammered pulling his trousers up.

"That's a big word for a tart Cas," Suzie unnecessarily explained.

Carol climbed from the floor and began to dress. "What? What d'yer think yer gonna catch off me Gus?"

"Aids, Syphilis, Gonorrhoea, Hepatitis, God knows!"

"You keep that up and you'll catch my knee in yer crotch."

"How do you know you haven't caught anything eh? Have you been medically examined?"

A tear welled in Carol's eye. "He's right yer knows Sooze. I could be contaminated. Best get yerself to the docs in the morning eh Gus? Don't know what yer've caught. I do knows one thing though. When yer given the all clear remember tonight 'cos it will probably be the last bit of cunt you see. Most girls ain't as charitable as me."

"What's that supposed to mean?"

"It means dick 'ead that you're a humourless, self-opinionated, arrogant, ignorant, ugly little runt, that's what."

Carol put on her shoes and told Jeff. "I'm leavin' now. I ain't stoppin' for no more insults."

Suzie already dressed added. "I don't blame yer gel. I'll come wiv yer."

"Where will you go this time of night?" Jeff asked anxious.

"Don't matter, just outa here."

"I can't drive girls, I've been drinking. If I get pulled that'll be my lot."

Suzie glared at him. "You stay with your chum. We've 'ad enough blokes for one night."

"You sure you don't mind?" He walked to the door with them. "I'll come if you want, but I could diffuse the situation. I mean it is all a misunderstanding isn't it?. Gus'll come around I'm sure."

"Yeah." Carol smiled up at the big lad." You stay wiv yer best mate, make sure he ain't too upset at bein' raped by a bug infested slut. You make sure he's all 'appy. Tuck 'im up in bed wiv a 'ot cocoa. Tell 'im a bed time story. Goldilocks and the three visitors should do it. Then jump into bed wiv 'im and make yer bloody night!" She stormed off.

"Prick!" Suzie hissed, then followed.

Figure 1 Chapter 9 Talk to Me Jane

10-Talk to Me Jane

Chains cracked as they tightened. The wooden cog and lever mechanism clicked ominously with every movement. A naked Jane Willet ground her teeth as the metal straps bit ever deeper into her hands and feet.

"Well sweet Jane, have you decided to divulge that address yet?"

"Go to hell," she spat.

"Another notch if you please Lisa."

"Nooo! Aaagh!"

"Beg your pardon?"

"I won't do no more. You'll get me into trouble." Lisa stepped away from the lever.

"Get you into trouble," Cork mimicked sarcastically. "You stupid bitch you are in trouble. Up to your scrawny neck."

"Not with the law I ain't. I won't go no further with this."

"Very well Lisa." Cork smiled. "Time I believe, to teach you a lesson in life."

A split second later Cork had her by the throat. He forced her backwards to a large wooden cross. Still holding her, stifling her breath, he growled. "Drop your pants girl."

Terrified, she loosened the jeans and let them fall.

"Knickers," Cork hissed, a demonic rage in his eyes.

Down they went.

"Jumper." He released his hold.

"Brassiere."

That having dropped to the floor Lisa stood naked, wishing she were anywhere else but there.

"Turn around Lisa."

She obeyed, shaking like a leaf.

Cork's hand pressed into her back and forced her forward. "Spread those legs woman!" he barked.

He strapped her ankles to the bottom half of the 'X', her feet under the hollows at the base of each upright.

"Reach for the sky." Cork secured her wrists to the uppermost points, leaving her stretched, her body taut.

"Now we'll show Miss Willet what she has in store. I'm going to whip you Lisa. I'm going to flay your back. Repay you for the bite you gave me."

"Please Mister Cork don't. Please don't. I beg you."

"Would you rather I used a precious bullet on your empty skull?"

Lisa began to sob. "Oh Gawd, I want my mum. All.....all I .....I ever did was ask you for a lift."

"Poor Lisa. Forget we tried to trade our cunt have we? Forget we bit your saviour's penis eh? Forgotten we punched him in the bollocks have we?" Corks voice rose in strength from sentence to sentence.

"I...I'm s...sorry," she howled, tears streaming down her face.

"You will be Lisa. You will be."

Jane threw her critical pennyworth in. "You see what you get young woman, for cohorting with a villain."

"I never did. That were all lies. He made me pretend that....Aaahh!" The first lash of the whip curled to her back, ripping into her pale skin, lashing her with a profound brutality.

The scourge struck for a second time. The awful whack echoing about the silence. Lisa screamed, she unable to bear the terrible pain.

Methodically he cut her back. Tiny trickles of crimson sources where the tip sliced. Lisa screamed and yelped with every mind rending lash, until as he reached the small of her back, then she fell silent.

"Lisa," Cork prompted.

No reply.

"Lisa," he urged a trifle louder.

Silence.

"LISA!" he bawled.

Still no reply.

"I do declare the damned milksop has fainted," Cork remarked, disgusted. He glanced about for a source of refreshing her, but water appeared unavailable in that 'cell'.

"Ah well she's not going anywhere. I'll finish her off later," he announced to nobody in particular.

He returned his attentions to the housekeeper. "Well sweet Jane, changed your mind?"

"You bullying cow pat. That poor girl. You'll pay dearly one day."

"Oh Jane, you talk such absolute tripe. I'm not paying for anything. They had me locked up. I escaped. I have killed one young man and I intend to dispose of two young tarts. If I have to torture you to death I'll do it. You see sweet Jane, personally I couldn't give a damn."

He stepped back and laid the whip to her taut behind, she refusing to satisfy his lust by yelping.

Cork lashed her again, her well shaped butt shimmering to the impact. Still no cry of anguish.

Taken aback by her resolve he growled caustically. "Hard nosed bint aren't you? I will tell you Jane I have the strength and all night available. I can flog you until the cock crows if necessary."

Jane sighed and turned her face away from him. Her father had said the same thing to her twenty four years before. Sixteen years old, he had accused her of having relations with a local farmer's boy and attempted to extricate a confession with a barber's strop.

Considering she had to fend the virile youth off in the hay loft to save her virtue, her treatment had been grossly unfair.

As Cork whipped her behind, her mind returned to that terrible time. She had been courting Alan Bickerstaffe for several weeks. He seemed a nice enough lad, seventeen, left school and working on his father's farm. Jane still at school going for her 'A' levels had felt the need for a boyfriend. All her mates were seeing someone. She worried about being left on the shelf.

Jane, a pretty teenager with a good figure had been a shy scholar, dressing down, with no idea of how to tempt the opposite sex. So at sixteen she had had no experience of boys.

Alan a friend of a girlfriend's boyfriend looked beyond the dowdy exterior and glimpsed the unseen body lurking beneath. He schemed to win her, change her and then have her.

The farmhand asked her out, his pockets full of money and a Honda motorcycle in his proud possession impressed the young Jane.

Insidiously he coerced her into wearing makeup, buying her clothes to suit him and not her. She had to apply the paint and dress away from home for if her father, a redoubtable martinet, had caught her she would have paid a dear price indeed.

On a balmy day in late August in nineteen seventy four, Alan walked her, charmed her and led her to the barn.

He seduced her in the hay loft. With passion all consuming he kissed and touched until his crotch ached, fit to burst. Jane nervous permitted him the embrace, believing that that was what sixteen-year old virgins did.

Her flimsy short cotton dress, showing an ample cleavage and plenty of thigh invoked a dreadful need in him.

His hand wandered to her breasts, feeling the firm full bosom through her dress and bra. She let that go.

Alan slid a hand beneath the covering and squeezed the pleasing tit, she found that peculiarly arousing.

Then he wandered beneath the hem and stroked her firm stockinged thighs. The tide rose.

Digits, hot and sweaty probed beneath the skimp panties, she made room for them. Slowly she was being taken but couldn't foresee the final outcome.

Alan was good, devious and cunning. He cajoled her from that flimsy dress, her laying in the hay, her underwear accentuating his ardour.

Acutely aroused herself, she permitted the removal of her bra, wishing only to be fondled, the act stimulating, increasing the thrill.

Even when he released his 'thingy', the first penis she had ever seen, she happily indulged him by fooling with it.

Alan asked to view her bottom, telling her that she had such a beautiful body he wanted to see it all. She rolled over, the lad removing her panties. She enjoyed his touch and kisses to that oh so sensitive and intimate area.

Then he declared he held a treat in store for her. Would she kneel on all fours. Overwhelmed by a carnal desire and excited tremendously she had done so, his hand stroking her arse. He dipped a finger, knowing just where to touch.

But when she sensed the attempted intrusion of something much larger she recoiled and pulled away. She sat staring, disbelieving. He knelt, that thing pointing at her.

"No," she hissed. "No Alan. I'm not ready."

"You can't say no, not now," he thundered. "Bloody hell! You've got me all het up."

"No Alan, you did that," she retorted.

"I'm sorry Jane, I've got to have you. You can't let me down now." He fell upon her, pushing her back, trying to get his penis in. She fought, bit and scratched. Finally, thankfully, she extricated herself from his grasp.

She hadn't had time to dress; she grabbed her dress and shoes and fled. Leaving an irate, pride damaged, frustrated boy behind. Unfortunately she left her underwear also.

Down the ladder she fled, rapidly putting on her dress and shoes at the bottom before running to where she had left her formal clothing. She then walked the three miles home, half expecting Alan to catch up to her. Half hoping he would and for him to apologise profusely.

Matters worsened. Alan's father found the undies the next day, her name clearly printed in the brassiere, in case of loss or theft at school. The pious farmer faced Alan with that evidence accusing. Alan lied saying she tried to seduce him, but he didn't want sex with that sort of girl. She, according to Alan had dashed off in a huff not bothering to dress properly.

So Alan's father approached hers telling him the sad tale, underwear provided as proof.

Jane had been summonsed, her father Victorian in attitude, asked her why her underclothes had been found in Mister Bickerstaffe's hay loft.

What could she say? Alan had tried to rape her? She had allowed him to strip her near naked and indulged in all those pre-sex activities. She remained sullen, silent, seething for Alan's cowardice, lies and deceit.

"If you do not provide me with suitable reason," her father insisted. "I shall have no alternative but to severely punish you."

Jane stared vacantly out of the window. Perhaps she deserved a beating. Perhaps she had done wrong. In future she would keep the hounds at bay.

"Very well girl. As you seem to enjoy disrobing before all and sundry, you can do so before me. Then young lady I shall spank you over my knee."

He waited patiently while she removed every stitch, his eyes not wavering, her embarrassment acute. She had not thought for one second that he might have been perverted in any shape or form. No she was sure his intention was purely to humiliate her. He had succeeded.

She had lain over his lap and he had spanked her. That had gone on for a seeming eternity. Oh it hadn't hurt too much at first, but by the time she had mentally counted forty her butt was really burning. From there on in that firm hand proved pure hell. Her backside so sore she wriggled and kicked, to which her father responded by beating her harder.

For a full five minutes he reddened her butt. When he finally let her up, she went sobbing to get her clothes.

"You'll dress when I say so Jane. I'm not finished with you yet, not by a long chalk," her father had decreed.

Much to her chagrin, Jane's father had forced her to lay over the end of their settee, her hot backside forced up for the strop he held with menace.

She remembered how much that had hurt her, her flesh and her pride. He had beat her remorselessly, the wide hard leather smacking her over and over, her bottom cheeks already so sore from his hand.

She had eventually shrieked as the pain mounted, went beyond her ability to sustain it, the leather searing her backside, Jane dreading the next.

Her father had ignored her pleas, her cries for mercy. He had beaten her backside until he had deemed her contrite.

But it still hadn't ended. With Jane barely able to stand he had produced a cane, telling her that she deserved the ultimate deterrent.

He had made her bend double, subjugated, her hot scarlet backside proffered for his rod. She would never forget those cuts. The severity etched in her for all time. After each violent stroke he permitted her thirty seconds to recompose herself, such was his brutality.

Twelve of those he had applied to her. A dozen that striped her so badly the marks remained for ten days.

Then he had made her stand facing the wall hands on her head. For a full half hour she had to endure, unable to soothe the fire in her behind, unable to conceal her embarrassment.

All the while her father had sucked on his pipe, doing his paperwork, his naked whipped daughter before him.

Now she was there again. Another sadist twenty four years on, he savouring the dance of her flesh.

Jane did not enjoy pain. Her tolerance though was noteworthy. She could frustrate Cork's efforts by receiving without complaint.

So Jane endured. Her buttocks coated in livid stripes, the skin sliced in places, blood smeared over the puffy flesh, she withstood.

Eventually Cork accepted she would not break too easily. "Perhaps I **was** right about you Jane. Maybe you do enjoy a bit of a slap after all."

Jane ignored him.

"Do you know Jane? I'm tired. I have had very little sleep of late. I'm going to get my head down for a few hours.

When I return Jane. Now I want you to think on this. Cogitate. You see that pillory over there. I'm going to put you in there Jane. And then woman I'm going to cut your bloody back to pieces.

You ponder on that while you lay there stretched. Goodnight sweet Jane."

"Before you go. I need to visit the toilet."

"Oh, do you now? See how long you can hold on. I mean it's not my house, my equipment, so I really don't give a damn Jane. Nighty night."

Cork left them. Jane taut upon the rack. Lisa slumped at the cross. He retired to the study, falling into a deep undisturbed sleep on the leather couch.

At daybreak he returned, a hot coffee in hand. As he opened the door he overheard the women talking.

Lisa was saying. "He's a vicious son of a bitch, completely off his trolley."

"Whatever he is I'll not tell him anything."

"Yer've got to Jane. If yer tell him what he wants to know he'll leave us alone. I can't take no more Jane. Look at me back. He's cut me to buggery. He won't stop there. God knows what he'll do next."

"You have to be brave Lisa. He'll have to give up sooner or later."

"He seemed very interested in puttin' a rope around yer neck yesterday. What if he decides to do that?"

"He won't learn anything if he kills me," Jane assured her.

"He'd probably get 'is mate the devil to send word back."

"Now ain't that the truth," Cork boomed. "I like that idea. The ultimate. To hang somebody. How about you first Lisa? To get in the swing of things eh?"

"No, please Mister Cork, don't, not that." She began to sob again.

"He's provoking you Lisa. Even he couldn't be that cruel."

"I could Jane. Oh I could."

Cork strolled about the room seeking, eventually coming up with a length of rope. "Do you know Lisa I'm getting quite excited at the prospect of seeing you swinging, gurgling, slowly turning blue."

"Jane!" she screamed. "He's gonna do it. He's really gonna 'ang me. For Christ's sake tell him where they are."

"He's not Lisa. He's all front."

Cork sat down whistling tunefully and set about making a hangman's noose. Completed, he looked for somewhere to suspend it. Not difficult in that type of room. There were suspension points in numerous places.

He callously threaded the rope through an eye bolt, secured to a ceiling beam and let the noose swing about head height, Lisa's head height.

Going back to Lisa, he whispered in her ear. "Well girl do you think Jane will save you? Or perhaps her little trio of perverts mean more to her? Anyway Lisa, it ain't all bad is it girl? I mean you get to meet your maker don't you? And you get away from me........For good."

He unstrapped her wrists, then re-secured them behind her with a pair of handcuffs. He then released her legs.

Having spent some six hours on the cross she could barely stand, let alone walk. Cork gave her time to regain her feelings.

Jane made an offer. "If I gave you an address, how could you be sure it would be the right one?"

"Simple Jane. I would take Lisa with me. If you lied I would return without her. You understand my drift? Then I would recommence my inquisition on you. I'm in no hurry Jane. I'll catch up one way or the other. They will eventually return home."

"I still don't believe you'll do it Cork."

"Oh, doubting Thomas. You still do not believe me capable of murder. I suppose I shall just have to demonstrate Jane. But do bear in mind. If you force me to kill the girl then I shall start peeling the hide from you. The death of a thousand cuts. Dwell on that."

Cork pushed Lisa to the waiting rope, she fighting against him, able to see that noose waiting for her pretty neck. Her legs gave from under her time and again, only to have Cork catch and lift her back up.

Then the noose tightened about her throat. Her eyes, red rimmed, stared enormous from ashen skin. Her lips trembled. Fear enveloped her; the mist of sheer terror hung chill to her trembling body.

"You think I'm bluffing still, don't you Jane? See if you still believe so when she starts to buck. When she gasps for air and there is none forthcoming. When her eyes bulge and her lips turn blue. When she stares with hatred at you Jane, for she knows you stole her life."

He pulled. The noose tightened. Lisa felt the rope's bite. "FOR GOD'S SAKE!" she screamed. "Tell him. Tell him you stupid fucking cow. I'm gonna die cos of you. Tell him.....Aaaaagh!

Her speech severed as Cork took her weight she started to rise, her toes desperate to keep contact with the floor.

Her face scarlet, eyes wide, tongue protruding she left the floor her legs kicking frantically.

"Stop it!" Jane screamed. "I'll tell you. For pity's sake let her down."

Cork held her suspended, Lisa's face puce. "So tell me sweet Jane."

"Dell Cove Cottage. Blithend road. Plymouth. God help me."

Lisa crumpled to the floor. Cork loosened the noose. "See how easy it was Jane. I told you you would tell me in the end. You could have saved yourself and poor Lisa here a lot of grief."

"You bastard!"

"Ain't that the truth," he agreed, tying the limp girl's ankles.

"Now Jane, I think I'll string you up. You seemed so content to let Lisa pay for your cussedness I think you should have a go. To be honest Jane I found the experience quite stimulating."

A hammering on the front door prevented him taking that matter any further. He waited silently to see what would transpire.

The banging persisted. "Not the postman me thinks," Cork whispered.

"Open up. Police," came the distant reply to his suspicions.

"Open up or we'll break the door down."

"Oh dear," Cork sighed. "Just when I was having such a wonderful time. Seems like I'll have to leave you for another day Jane. I should silence you permanently really, but I haven't the time it seems. I'll come back though, woman. I'll finish what I started at some other time. *Au revoir.*" His fist struck her sharply on the temple rendering her unconscious.

Cork sped from the cell, to the sound of police shoulders on the front door.

As the door finally gave and the two detectives fell through the opening, so Cork slipped out of a window. The cops on a crusade hurtled through the passageway, kicking doors open and shouting for recognition. Cork quietly opened their car door and smashed the two way. He then opened the bonnet and stole the leads.

The Jaguar's engine fired he sped away in a pool of condensing exhaust for Plymouth.

Some five minutes later the two plain clothes policemen discovered the unconscious forms of Jane and Lisa.

"Good God!" detective sergeant Peters exclaimed on seeing the pair. Releasing Jane, his mind quickly assessed the situation. His cohort detective constable Merrow knelt beside Lisa carefully untying her ropes.

"A pound to a penny it was Cork," Peters bet. "I wonder how long the bastard's been gone."

"Look at the marks on this girl's neck. It looks like he has tried to strangle her," Merrow surmised.

120

"Over by that...... Fuck me! What sort of place is this?" the sergeant shocked, asked. "There by that pillory or whatever, a hangman's noose. Get on the radio and order an ambulance."

Merrow ran out, returning a few minutes later. "Ambulance is on its way and Cork, if it was him left ten minutes ago."

"How do you know that?"

"Because he smashed our set and stole the H.T. leads. I had to ring on my mobile."

"Fuck! Didn't you lock the bloody car?"

"Sorry sarge," Merrow replied picking the naked Lisa up in his arms. "Nice looking girl," he remarked.

"God! There's going to be hell to pay over this and all you can think of is the girl's looks. Get her on the couch in the front of the house Merrow and stop ogling her body. And cover her up for Christ's sake."

Merrow grinned. "Yes Guv."

Peters followed carrying Jane.

"How long?" Peters asked panting with his burden.

"Ambulance? About fifteen minutes they reckoned."

"I....I tell you..... The more I see of this case, the..... sicker..... I get," Peters gasped. "First he blows a hole in that poor cunt's head."

"You don't know for certain sarge."

"I know. All I have to do is prove it. Then he does this to these innocent women. I tell you I'm going to enjoy nailing his arse."

Peters dumped his charge and covered her with a coat. "Go get their clothes. I think I saw them laying about. Better call the D.I. and get forensics down here." He staggered to the window and leant on the sill exasperated. "I tell you Merrow when..... When..... Where's that bloody Jag gone?"

"Jag guv?"

"Yeah. When we came in there was a Jag parked outside. Fuck! Cork! Where's that mobile of yours?"

Peters made a number of calls. An all points was immediately sent to all squad cars in the area.

Cork, inveterate policeman, drove the back roads, lanes and cart tracks of his native soil aware he had to keep a low profile or ditch the motor.

Figure 1 Chapter 11 Closing In

11-Closing In

Some two hours later in a casualty ward in Plymouth Jane finally roused. Groggy she immediately asked how she had arrived there.

"Ambulance," replied the nurse assigned to her.

"Yes, but who found me?" She was suffering from a mild concussion and amnesia.

"The police I believe."

"I must talk with them now," Jane insisted.

"Not now. See the doctor first. You've had a nasty bang to the head."

"Nurse, are the police here now?"

"Outside."

"Then get them now. It is literally a matter of life and death."

Two minutes later she was telling detective sergeant Peters where Cork had headed. In fact where he probably was at that very moment.

A half dozen units, including an armed response unit were on the road to Dell Cove Cottage within minutes. Peters stayed with Jane to question her tactfully.

"You know he has a gun don't you?"

"Yes Miss Willet we do. Now have no fear, he will be apprehended very shortly."

"I had to tell him you see."

"Now don't worry yourself. The man is an utter lunatic. You did the right thing."

"How is the girl? Lisa."

"She's conscious. She'll be okay. Superficial wounds that's all."

"How did you find me, us?"

"Routine enquiry. We went to Miss Widney's flat in London. Circumstances there led us to believe she had reason to visit Miss Dixon. We were attempting to find her to warn her that Cork may well have been hunting her." Peters didn't mention Wayne's corpse.

"You see we tracked him from his escape in Farnham to London. The chances were he was out for revenge."

"But how did you know we were in mortal danger? Last I remember you were threatening to break the door down."

"We had reason to believe Cork was inside ma'am. We could afford to take no chances."

"Oh those poor mites. He's going to kill them both. Suzanne and Ms Widney. Suzanne's heavily pregnant as well."

"Are you going to answer that bloody door Gus?" Jeff yelled from the warmth of his bed.

"My head's banging Jeff. I feel right ill. Get it will you? It's probably Suzanne and slack Alice come crawling back."

That seemed the only possibility. Jeff slipped on a dressing gown and bounded eagerly down the stairs. He had been worried. He should have gone with them. But they were back now, that was all that mattered.

He threw open the door. No girls. A tall, stocky, pot bellied stranger awaited his appearance.

"Can't piss about," the man began. "No time. Where is Widney?"

"S..sorry?" Jeff gasped, not comprehending.

"Where's Widney? Don't fuck me about. She here?" He pushed pass Jeff and nosed into the sitting room.

"Where the fuck do you think......" Jeff protested. A revolver answered his half asked question.

"Where's the tart dick head? I've got a bullet for her."

Jeff could not grasp the import. Even with the gun pointed at his chest. One just doesn't expect that sort of thing to happen. Especially at nine forty five in the morning, in somebody else's house.

"Who are you?" he asked stupidly.

"I'm the man that is going to take that miserable wretches life. Now where is the whore?"

"She's not here," a sickly Gus interrupted.

"A likely story."

"Honest, she left with her friend last night. I don't know where they've gone."

Cork growled and then roared, smacking his forehead in frustration. Jeff lurched forward trying to grab the gun hand. He met with the barrel knocking all sensation from his body. A crack on the forehead and he slumped to the floor.

Cork stared insanely at Gus. "Now you. You tell me where they are, or I swear I'll blow your fucking brains away." He levelled the revolver at Gus' forehead.

"They left mister. Like I said one, maybe two this morning. We had a row. Me and Carol. She's a right scrubber. They were on foot. I don't know where they went. Honest I don't."

"Then make an educated guess. If that is not beyond you."

Gus held out his hands in supplication. "Please, I don't know."

"Did they order a taxi?"

"No."

"Where would you go on a freezing night at two in the morning and on foot?"

"The cove. There's a motel there."

"Thank you!" Cork laid the weak Gus out with one blow to the jaw. Then ripped the phone from the wall as he left.

Cork reached his car to hear the distant wail of a siren. He smiled, turned the car around and waited. A police car hurtled over the brow of the hill to find Cork's Jag occupying all of the road. Cork slammed the accelerator down. Black smoke balled from the tyres. The oncoming police car had no choice. They veered, his the curb and lost all control, sliding sideways past an evasive Cork.

The Jaguar screamed off, engine revving like a banshee. Cork was gone.

He had passed the motel on his way to Dell Cove Cottage, so he knew exactly where it was. He passed another three police vehicles a half mile down the road. Fortunately for him they had been directed to Gus' cottage on an 'armed and dangerous' call. There had been no mention of him or his car.

The Jag slid to a halt in the motel car park. Cork walked directly to the foyer. Using his profound knowledge of police attitudes he spoke to the clerk, a mere slip of a girl who didn't bother checking him out.

"Detective sergeant John Cork." He introduced himself with an outrageous arrogance. "I believe a Miss Dixon and a Miss Widney booked in here last night. It would have been in the early hours."

"Hold on sir, I'll check." She read the register. "Yes room fourteen."

"Are they in now?" His hand gripped the pistol in his coat pocket.

The girl checked the keys; fourteen was on the hook. "No sir. Oh I remember now. A blond and a brunette. The dark haired one looked pregnant."

"Did she now? Have you any idea where they might have gone?"

"I think they went for a walk sir. An hour since. The beach I think it was."

"Thanks." Cork ran from the building. The whole world seemed to reel to the sound of distant sirens. He stared at the Jaguar. He had no time for that. If he tried to leave by car they would nail him for sure.

Remarkably fit, he ran around the building, across the lawns and down onto the beach.

There! Half a mile away he spotted his quarry, walking away from him, beneath the lee of the cliffs.

He ran. A hundred yards on he began to blow. Three hundred and he was panting hard. He glanced over his shoulder; blue uniforms were on the beach. *'Blast!'* he thought. They had spotted his car.

"Is we going back to the cottage Cas? Or is we catchin' the train 'ome?"

"Don't know. Don't care. Jumped up little toe rag. No rush is there?"

"Nah girl. Got me credit card ain't I? Lady of means yer knows."

"Yer a real mate anyhow. 'Ere ain't that bobbies runnin' up behind us?"

"Gawd Cas! He ain't made a rape charge 'as he?"

"There's gotta be a 'alf dozen of 'em. There're chasin' that geezer look. D'yer know from 'ere it looks like Cork."

"Yer got Cork on the brain gel. He's locked up ain't he?"

Carol grabbed Suzanne's arm. "Christ! I think I just shit meself Sooze. That is Cork. Jesus fuckin' H Christ. Leg it."

Their worst nightmare was within four hundred yards and running like a demon. The girls fled for the cliffs, a stepped pathway led to the top from there. The beach at that point gave way to the sea. They could see policemen on the edge, some ways off but making for the same summit.

They hit the bottom step; Suzanne fell to her knees. "Go on Cas, go! I can't make it. I can't get up there. Go on I'll be all right."

"I can't leaves yer gel. I can't."

Cork paused, raised his arm, a jet of fire erupted from what he held pointed at them. A distant crack sounded, the emissary of death ricocheted from the surrounding rocks.

"Go Cas. For God's sake go. It's you he wants, not me."

Carol held Suzie's hand, squeezed it and as Cork started running again, so did she, climbing the steps like a young Gazelle.

Cork reached Suzanne; she still squatted on the bottom step. He held the gun up, pointing it at her head. "So you're pregnant are you slut?" Suzanne nodded slowly. "Do you know who the father is?"

"Course I does."

"Then may your child enjoy all life's pleasures. It's a shame the child won't have a mother worth a damn, but at least that offspring will never be influenced by that blond trollop." He pointed up the cliff. Then he was running up after Carol.

Suzanne watched him go. Police were everywhere, but not close enough to stop him.

Carol reached the summit some fifty feet above the beach. She ran toward the uniforms in the distance, the police approaching from the opposite direction from which she had come.

The sea crashed against the rocks below her. Another crack and a bullet tore up the grass beside her. She stopped. Somehow she didn't want to be shot in the back.

Carol slowly turned to face Cork. He walked up to her, gun hand hung by his side. He moved in close, until she stared up into his hard cold eyes.

"If I get real close Carol they won't chance a shot. And if I hold the barrel tight to your side like this they are even less likely to risk it," he explained breathing heavy. You didn't really think I'd let you get away with trying to kill me, did you?"

"If I'd wanted to kill you, I'd 'ave done so." Carol gasped, equally out of breath.

"Oh sharpshooter are we?"

"I could 'ave killed yer easy."

"Then why didn't you?"

"Cos that would 'ave dragged me down to your level."

"Which is?"

"I don't 'ave to tell yer. Yer knows yer the scum of the earth."

"And you aren't I suppose?"

"I'll stand up and be accounted for come judgement day."

"That time is very close Carol."

"Then get it done wiv."

"So quick? I've waited, schemed and planned for this day. All I've thought about since the Pegasus is taking your miserable life."

"Are yer ready to meet your maker as well? The devil that is."

"What makes you think I will?" Cork looked up. The police were all around him, holding a line sixty yards off.

"You shoots me. They'll shoot you. Stop yer pumpin' a second round in."

"So my time is up as well is it?"

"I reckon so. Course yer could just let me go. I mean yer ain't done for no one yet 'ave yer?"

"As it 'appens gel, I done for yer old mucker Wayne."

"Eh?"

"Yes my dear. I blew him away. I thought I'd do you a favour like."

"You bastard! Poor Wayne. Why kill him?"

"It was you I wanted and he got in my way."

"Cork." A distorted voice grated through a megaphone. "Put down the gun Cork and put your hands in the air."

Cork ignored the challenge. "Last time we were this close I had my prick up you, not that that would have bothered you."

"Oh it did. I should have done for yer. Rid the earth of your vile face."

"Cork! Surrender now!" The robotic voice hailed him again.

"Oh fuck off!" Cork raised the handgun and loosed two rounds. "That's D.I. Savage. He always was an ignorant peasant. Seems he's getting impatient. No more words. No more games, only the silence of the grave now girl."

In one swift movement he heaved Carol onto his shoulder and stepped off the cliff.

Suzanne who had managed the top saw him. Saw her beloved Carol and screamed. "Noooo!"

They were gone.

Suzanne fell to the ground huddling the pain in her abdomen. She sobbed uncontrollably. "Oh Carol," she wailed.

Original printed cover picture

Academy Incorporated

- *turning fantasy into reality* -

Does a reform school where adult boys, girls and special girls relive or rewrite their schooldays appeal? Or maid training for work with us at Muir Academy or as historical role-play with real spanking and bondage, or elsewhere? Or would you like to be a Master, Mistress, slave, human pony or puppy in that village? Or do you want mail-order books, magazines, implements, audio and video tapes, adult-size school or maid uniform?

We help one and all to do such things, men and women, 18 to 80s, married, couple or single; cross-dressers, transsexuals, heterosexuals, bisexuals, homosexuals, Dominants, switches, submissives, the short, tall, fat or thin, beginner or those who've done it all, able- bodied or otherwise, any race or religion. Discreetly too, and in safety, since 1987.

For free info.

contact:

PO Box 135, Hereford, HR2 7WL, UK

www.tawse.com, email: guy@tawse.com

or ring 01432 343100

Lightning Source UK Ltd.
Milton Keynes UK
UKHW021959090223
416682UK00013B/1392